MAKING FRIENDS WITH DARKNESS

MAKING FRIENDS WITH DARKNESS

Finding Spiritual Healing After Trauma or Loss

NICK HAMILTON

Copyright © 2025 by Nick Hamilton
All rights reserved.
Printed in the United States of America

979-8-3845-0800-7

Published by B&H Publishing Group
Brentwood, Tennessee

Dewey Decimal Classification: 616.85
Subject Heading: POST-TRAUMATIC STRESS
DISORDER \ ANXIETY \ STRESS (PSYCHOLOGY)

Unless otherwise noted all Scripture is taken from the Christian Standard Bible. Copyright © 2017 by Holman Bible Publishers. Used by permission. Christian Standard Bible®, and CSB® are federally registered trademarks of Holman Bible Publishers, all rights reserved.

Scripture references marked NLT are taken from the New Living Translation, copyright © 1996, 2004, 2015 by Tyndale House Foundation. Used by permission of Tyndale House Publishers, Inc., Carol Stream, Illinois 60188. All rights reserved.

Scripture references marked NIV are taken from the New International Version®, NIV® Copyright ©1973, 1978, 1984, 2011 by Biblica, Inc.® Used by permission. All rights reserved worldwide.

Scripture references marked NKJV are taken from the New King James Version®. Copyright © 1982 by Thomas Nelson. Used by permission. All rights reserved.

Scripture references marked ESV are taken from the English Standard Version. ESV® Text Edition: 2016. Copyright © 2001 by Crossway Bibles, a publishing ministry of Good News Publishers.

Cover design by Darren Welch Design. Cover image by Bitter/istock and Darren Welch Design. Author photo by Simon Hurst.

1 2 3 4 5 6 • 28 27 26 25

Dedicated to Karen, Emily, Nathan, and Noah
who have lived with me through the many journeys
that led to the writing of this book.

Acknowledgments

WITH A BOOK OF THIS type, there are more people who need to be thanked for their contributions than can ever be acknowledged. However, that does not mean that one should not try. First, I want to thank my loving wife, Karen, and our three children Emily, Nathan, and Noah. The four of you endured the life of a military chaplain for nearly twenty years. That included new houses, new schools, new communities, and new churches every three years. It also included long periods of separation, some that came with the uncertainty of whether I would come home. From the bottom of my heart, thank you for being there for me as I tried to minister to others in places and circumstances that were often challenging.

There are also several college and seminary professors who helped shape my thoughts and ministry practices over the years: Dr. Dick Rader and Dr. Tom Wilks at Oklahoma Baptist University and Dr. Clint Ashley, Dr. Kon Yang, Dr. Gregg Watson, Dr. David McCormick, and Dr. Jeff Iorg at Golden Gate Baptist Seminary, now known as Gateway Seminary of the Southern Baptist Convention. It was Dr. Mike Baird's Old Testament Poetry class at Grand Canyon University in the Fall 1993 semester that was the genesis of some of the ideas that would eventually become this book.

There are several chaplains deserving thanks as well: VA chaplain Henry Peterson, who introduced me to the writings of Walter Brueggemann and their significance in dealing with PTSD; Navy chaplain colleagues Bruce Crouterfield, John Miyahara, Tim Springer, and Glenn Orris; and clinical pastoral educator Nancy Dietsch. Thank you to the entire team of chaplains at Baptist Health in Montgomery for their support in my writing and, specifically, for my administrative assistant, Michele Creel, who read the first draft of many of these pages.

To Baptist Health CEO Russ Tyner, thank you for your trust in my leadership throughout the COVID-19 pandemic. Your support was unlike any that I had previously experienced.

Finally, thank you again to Dr. Jeff Iorg, who believed in this project and introduced me to the publishing team at B&H Publishing, and to Dr. Jim Wilson for your encouragement to write! Thank you especially to my editor at B&H Publishing, Matt Hawkins, whose support and encouragement have been first-class.

Contents

Introduction. 1

How to Read This Book 5

Chapter 1: Making Friends with Darkness 7

Chapter 2: Where Are You? 28

Chapter 3: Safe Space 50

Chapter 4: Guidance in the Wilderness. 68

Chapter 5: You DO Know! 90

Chapter 6: Choices 110

Chapter 7: New Normal 130

Chapter 8: Expectations. 149

Chapter 9: I Only Thought I Knew You 168

Epilogue. 186

Appendix 187

Notes 192

About the Author. 197

Introduction

"Darkness is my closest friend."
Psalm 88:18b NLT

SEPTEMBER 11, 2001. THE WARS in Afghanistan and Iraq. The 2004 South Asian tsunami. Hurricane Katrina. The global financial meltdown. The COVID-19 pandemic. Russia's invasion of Ukraine. An economy on the brink of failure with the greatest jump in inflation in nearly a half century. That's all just in the first two decades of the twenty-first century. All of this is added to the "routine" pain that we see in our world on a regular basis. Suffering like murder, rape and sexual assault, cancer, car accidents, heart attacks, Alzheimer's, global hunger and poverty, abuse, neglect, human trafficking, divorce—the list keeps going, just like the Energizer bunny. Add it all up: We live in a dark world.

Sure, there are good people who are trying to be a light in such a darkened world. The work they do is heroic and makes a significant difference for many people. However, I'd like to talk about darkness. Most people want to move past darkness. Ignore it. Pretend that it doesn't exist or at least paint a nice face on darkness and move on. But for many people, darkness just won't go away. Their lives have been forever altered by some horrific event, and they will never be the same again.

May I invite you on a journey? If you have read this far, you probably already know what it feels like to experience darkness. My desire is to offer not just a path through the darkness, but a way to get in touch with the darkness you are experiencing in a way that makes it less scary, in a way that will help you be able to say, "Yes, this is what happened to me," and no longer be shocked by it or afraid of it.

For me, this has been a lifelong journey. In my late teens and early twenties I went through several bouts of depression that were never diagnosed. Not only were they never diagnosed, but I also tried my best to never let anyone know about them. I did what so many other people do: I painted a nice face on my life so that no one would know that anything was wrong. The issues that sparked this depression for me were issues that nearly everyone struggles with in their late teens and early twenties: relationship issues, direction in life, and identity.

Then, I reconnected with my faith. From ages seventeen to twenty-one, I had abandoned the Christian faith of my youth. But somehow, when I reconnected, it all felt new. It felt as though the pieces of my life were all beginning to come together. I had new and deeper friendships than I had ever experienced, the direction I had longed for in life began to come into focus, and I started to become more comfortable in my own skin.

A few years later, I took a class in college in Hebrew wisdom literature. I remember thinking, *If only the world understood these texts, they would have a much better framework for thinking about pain in our world.* Such thoughts came from the idea that, for many people, the evil that exists in our world becomes a reason

INTRODUCTION

to not believe in God. I thought that those texts in particular would, perhaps, help restore people's trust in God.

In the years that followed, I became a military chaplain. I served on an aircraft carrier on 9/11, deployed with US Marines to Iraq, and served inside the detention facility in Guantanamo Bay, Cuba. For nearly twenty years I walked with US Sailors and Marines during some of their toughest and darkest times. I listened to their stories and tried to help them make sense of life in the aftermath and—when possible—help them find God in what they had experienced.

When I retired from the military, I thought I was done with that kind of work, only to find myself leading a team of hospital chaplains through the global pandemic of COVID-19. We did our best to help families communicate with those who were dying when no one was allowed into the hospital; we gowned up and went into COVID rooms alongside other healthcare professionals; and we encouraged exhausted staff. This was added to the daily grind of tragedies like heart attacks, car accidents, and shootings.

What I offer in these pages is the fruit of those thirty years of counseling others through the darkness. My hope is for this book to become a part of your journey to come to terms with whatever form of darkness has descended upon your life. More than that, I hope you will be able to find God in the middle of whatever darkness in which you find yourself.

How to Read This Book

SINCE YOU ARE READING THIS book, first let me say, "Congratulations!" You have taken a huge step in dealing with the pain, hurt, and sorrow related to grief or the traumatic events of your life. Because this is such a huge step, and because this book addresses sensitive wounds, I want to provide some guidance about how to read this book and what to expect. Second, please pace yourself. You may get emotional as you read, so read it at a pace that works for you. This book is not intended to be read in one sitting. It is meant to be a companion for you as your journey through life takes you back to places. Go at your own pace. If at any time you find yourself overwhelmed, put the book down and pick it up when you are ready again.

I mentioned above that this book is meant to be a companion, but what does that mean in practical terms? It means, simply, that it is not meant as a replacement for therapy. If you have a counselor whom you trust, great! Let them know that you are reading this book to augment what you are doing in your counseling sessions. If you have never seen a counselor, I encourage you to reach out and talk to someone, particularly now, as you begin to read.

Also, please keep an open mind. You may feel you do not have use for God, or church, or religion at this time. My hope is, at some point, you may look back through everything and say something like, "I thought God had abandoned me completely and, quite frankly, wondered if there was a God. Now, I realize that He was with me through it all." For now, though, I'm grateful you're here and willing to explore this book as part of your healing.

Finally, while we spend most of this book on emotional and spiritual counsel, occasionally there is a need to explain clinical terms, or how therapists describe the experience of you or someone you love. There are a couple of terms that will be helpful to know up front. The first is *PTSD*, or Post-Traumatic Stress Disorder. In pop culture, this term is frequently overused or even abused. PTSD is a diagnosable mental health condition and is defined by the American Psychiatric Association's fifth edition of *The Diagnostic and Statistical Manual (DSM-5)*. For the full *DSM-5* definition of PTSD, please see the appendix.

The second term worth defining at this point is *moral injury*. Moral injury is a term that describes the moral and ethical conflict that is often the result of witnessing horrifying events. The term originated from psychologists who were treating Vietnam veterans. They discovered that, in many cases, there was a moral aspect of an event that went beyond the definition of PTSD. Researchers began to delve into the subject and, as they did, coined the term *moral injury*. The two most prominent definitions of moral injury are also included in the appendix.

Chapter 1

Making Friends with Darkness

"Darkness is my closest friend."
Psalm 88:18b NLT

PAIN EXISTS IN OUR WORLD. Darkness is a part of life. Let those two phrases sink in for a moment. While pain and dark times are inevitably part of the human experience, none of us wants to go through such times. Physical pain is the body's way of letting us know that something is wrong—that we should avoid whatever is causing us pain. Our natural reaction to avoidance also applies to us mentally, emotionally, and spiritually. Western culture compounds this. For much of the modern era, Western culture has lauded those with a positive outlook on life and happy disposition. The British talk about keeping a "stiff upper lip," and here in the US, there is an adage that, "Nobody wants to be around a sourpuss." Yet deep emotions like fear, loneliness, sadness, depression, and anger are a part of life. Most people don't like those emotions. They don't want to experience them and especially do not want to witness others as they experience them.

As a chaplain, I have often been surprised at how few people are able to stay engaged with, and really listen to, someone as they are experiencing grief. But when someone is going through a tough time, what they need most is someone to be there with them. I learned this lesson the hard way in my late twenties. My wife and I had been married for just over a year when her dad was diagnosed with prostate cancer. The news was difficult for the family. A few hours after we learned about it, I tried to get my wife to "snap out of it," to "cheer up," because I, like so many, was uncomfortable with difficult emotions. It was an insensitive move and helped me to begin to understand how to be present during tough times.

As you can imagine, my desire to put difficult emotions away is not unique. It happens all too often—just at the moment when people need someone around them the most, friends and family choose to let people be alone. Sometimes this is a well-intentioned desire to give people their privacy. Often it is simply a way to get away from the heavy and intense feelings of the other person—because such feelings are hard. The result is that people can easily feel abandoned or betrayed in their times of deepest need. Add to this sense of abandonment the idea that people often see evil and pain in our world as evidence that there is no God. Put it all together and, for many people, the deepest points of their lives make them feel not only abandoned by family and friends, but by God as well. Perhaps you have been there. Grief, loss, and trauma are all a part of life. But those parts of life are difficult and can feel impossible to get through.

MAKING FRIENDS WITH DARKNESS

These feelings are not new. The psalms of ancient Israel capture many of these laments in what some have called The Psalms of Disorientation.[1] One of those is Psalm 88. Before you read it, take a deep breath and sit comfortably in your chair. Then, imagine the worst moment of your life. Now, read these words with all the emotion you can muster:

> O LORD, God of my salvation,
>> I cry out to you by day.
>> I come to you at night.
> Now hear my prayer;
>> listen to my cry.
> For my life is full of troubles,
>> and death draws near.
> I am as good as dead,
>> like a strong man with no strength left.
> They have left me among the dead,
>> and I lie like a corpse in a grave.
> I am forgotten,
>> cut off from your care.
> You have thrown me into the lowest pit,
>> into the darkest depths.
> Your anger weighs me down;
>> with wave after wave you have engulfed
>> me. *Interlude*
>
> You have driven my friends away
>> by making me repulsive to them.
> I am in a trap with no way of escape.
>> My eyes are blinded by my tears.

MAKING FRIENDS WITH DARKNESS

Each day I beg for your help, O Lord;
    I lift my hands to you for mercy.
Are your wonderful deeds of any use to the
    dead?
    Do the dead rise up and praise you?
    Interlude

Can those in the grave declare your unfailing
    love?
    Can they proclaim your faithfulness in the
    place of destruction?
Can the darkness speak of your wonderful
    deeds?
    Can anyone in the land of forgetfulness
    talk about your righteousness?
O Lord, I cry out to you.
    I will keep on pleading day by day.
O Lord, why do you reject me?
    Why do you turn your face from me?

I have been sick and close to death since my
    youth.
    I stand helpless and desperate before your
    terrors.
Your fierce anger has overwhelmed me.
    Your terrors have paralyzed me.
They swirl around me like floodwaters all day
    long.
    They have engulfed me completely.

> You have taken away my companions and
> loved ones.
> Darkness is my closest friend. (NLT)

Emotion

Psalm 88 captures the raw emotion of someone who has experienced tragedy or difficulty in life. It does not put a nice bow on everything. The writer just lets it all out: the hurt, the anger, and even the accusations that God has not only allowed him to be in his situation but has intentionally left him there. The conclusion? "Darkness is my closest friend."

Several years ago I was leading a spirituality support group for veterans who had been diagnosed with Post-Traumatic Stress Disorder (PTSD). I decided to read Psalm 88 to the group. When I finished, I asked the group for reactions. One World War II veteran said, "It sounds like he's in deep $#!^." This veteran had instinctively connected with the emotions of Psalm 88 (NLT). Look back at some of them:

> "I am forgotten, cut off from your care" (v. 5b);
> "Your anger weighs me down . . ." (v. 7a);
> "I stand helpless and desperate before your terrors. Your fierce anger has overwhelmed me. Your terrors have paralyzed me." (vv. 15b–16)

The feelings described are those of helplessness, desperation, and being forgotten, which lead to other feelings of being weighed down, overwhelmed, and paralyzed. But notice what is not present. There is no judgment about these feelings. They are expressed as a matter of fact. Perhaps the ancient world was better at expressing grief related to tragedy than we are. Far too often in the modern world, particularly in Western Christianity, such emotions are looked down upon—even viewed as indicative of a person having no faith, having lost their faith in God, or worse, seen as blasphemous. I recently met a man who admitted to looking down on people who felt abandoned by God.

But trauma, grief, and loss *do* leave a person feeling overwhelmed, weighed down, and helpless. These are the feelings often described by many people who suffer from PTSD, depression, and other forms of loss or mental health disorders. They are natural reactions to the abnormal situation in which people find themselves in the wake of horrific events.

The veteran's group that I described above was thankful to be able to talk together about their emotions and experiences of war. Why? Talking about their experiences with others who had been through something similar helped them feel less forgotten. Consider for a moment how their experiences would make someone feel. Think about the helplessness, desperation, and sense of being forgotten. All of these veterans knew what it was like to fear for their lives. They had all known the sudden loss of friends in war. They had each experienced the horrors of waking up in the middle of the night in a cold sweat after dreaming, yet again, about their combat experiences. They each knew what it was like to be constantly looking over their shoulders, scanning for threats. They understood the scorn of loved ones who just could not cope with their hypervigilance. They lived daily with haunting memories and what-ifs such as, "Would my friend still be alive if the lieutenant wouldn't have been so incompetent?" They understood what it was like to be going about their normal lives and suddenly have something trigger them in a way that they were instantly transported back to the moment of their trauma as if they were reliving it right then.

Because of those shared experiences, there was natural camaraderie among the veterans. It helped them to feel less alone. Those who deal with significant challenges often feel alone because there are so few people around them who understand their stories, and fewer who understand their feelings in relation to what they have experienced. All of this stands to reason. It is impossible to have any idea what another person is feeling and experiencing unless you have walked in their footsteps. Even then, you can only relate to similar shared experiences.

Take, for example, the experience of the Vietnam veteran. Upon arrival "in country," he is designated the FNG—a term of derision for new arrivals whose life expectancy is often short. Those who live through the first month of combat are only then accepted by the unit as someone who could pull their weight and not get others killed. Over the next year, there will be daily patrols in the jungle and regular firefights; the loss of friends and buddies comes all too regularly. Time and location begin to fade away as the otherworldly experience of life in that place becomes the only reality known. There is occasional talk about "back in the world," meaning home. But it is as far distant emotionally and spiritually as it is in miles.

Then one day someone comes along and says, "Your DEROS (Date Estimated Return from Overseas) is up." Within twenty-four hours you are on a plane back to the States. Within forty-eight hours you may have had the experience of being spit upon by war protesters. Within seventy-two hours you are eating mashed potatoes at your mom's table, and within ninety-six hours, your dad is saying, "Okay, now that you are back, it's time to get a job." All the while your mind is on the buddies you lost and on those you left behind, wondering what is happening to them. There may be gratitude for surviving, but more likely there is an intense guilt for feeling like you abandoned your brothers. There is anger, confusion, grief, and a myriad of other feelings that are so overwhelming—but you don't know how to begin describing those thoughts and feelings to others. You may try once or twice, but the reactions you get cause you to stop trying. You are feeling so alone.

A young Marine and veteran of war in Afghanistan once described to me what the author of Psalm 88 was getting at when he spoke of feeling helpless, desperate, and forgotten. Specifically, this young man felt cut off from God's care. He said that while he was in Afghanistan, he was the guy in his squad who would lead others in prayer before going "outside the wire." He said, "We prayed that we wouldn't get hit [by an improvised explosive device (IED)] and we got hit; we prayed that everyone would be safe, and we still lost guys." His conclusion was that God could not exist because, if He did, He certainly should have answered their prayers. As a result, he turned away from the Christian faith of his childhood and struggled to make sense of a life in which he could no longer believe in God. This young man's story demonstrates the unfortunate reality that sometimes bad things happen in our world—things that leave people feeling forgotten and isolated from God and others. Traumas are so overwhelming that they cause them to question their core assumptions of life and leave them feeling alone.

Arguments

But it is not just about getting in touch with our emotions. At the heart of the matter are circumstances and problems that create these emotions in the first place. Notice the six questions that the author of Psalm 88 (NLT) asks God:

1. Are your wonderful deeds of any use to the dead? (v. 10a)
2. Do the dead rise up and praise you? (v. 10b)
3. Can those in the grave declare your unfailing love? (v. 11a)
4. Can they proclaim your faithfulness in the place of destruction? (v. 11b)
5. Can the darkness speak of your wonderful deeds? (v. 12a)
6. Can anyone in the land of forgetfulness talk about your righteousness? (v. 12b)

If you were to sum up these questions, they all have one remarkable theme and boil down to a single question: "God, what good am I to You if I am dead?" You can almost hear someone saying, "What good are the great stories of Your miracles and Your activity if I'm dead? If I'm dead, I can't worship or praise You; I can't talk about how great Your love is! The dead can't talk about such things."

Psalm 88 surfaces two important issues: first, the universal human experience of wondering where God is during seasons of tragedy and pain (see chapter 2). The other is the second-guessing of God. A more polite way to say it is wondering where God's miracles are when we experience our own seasons of distress and grief.

These questions describe the gut-wrenching experiences of life; the times when you collapse on the floor and scream, "Oh, God!" But no words follow. Then days, weeks, months, or years later you find you are still in the same place. No answers to why tragedy struck and the void of loss remains. You begin to ask, quietly at first, and then more insistently, "God, what happened? I believed in You—I trusted in You—and now this?" But there are always more questions than answers. Just like the writer of the psalm, you are left sitting alone in the darkness wondering about everything in life.

Has that ever been your experience? You are going through a particularly difficult time in life and you pray for a miracle, and nothing happens. You pray harder—and still nothing. You begin wondering why God is not answering. You may say something such as: "If God can part the Red Sea, why can He not help with my situation?" When there has been a trauma, this question is even more acute, more intense: "God, why didn't You prevent the [fill-in-the-blank] from happening?"

Many people asked this question in the days and weeks following 9/11. Churches and synagogues around the US were more crowded than they had been at any point in recent memory. There was a searching—a longing—to understand what had happened. Many were angry and asked why God had not prevented such a horrific tragedy. Soon, however, the influx of people into places of worship seemed to end. It was as if people had sought out God in the aftermath of their trauma and tragedy, but left feeling disappointed when there were no answers to why God had allowed such a horrific event and did not prevent it. The reality is that the world had forever changed! Almost three thousand people died that day. Untold numbers were traumatized as they watched the planes hit the towers. It seemed as though the only answers were related to finding those who had plotted and planned the attack. People seemed to give up on understanding *why* from a larger perspective and were content with security protocols and investigations that would reveal who was responsible.

The questions of the writer of Psalm 88 remain; here is my paraphrase: "God, where are You when I'm suffering?" "God, I've heard all of the Bible stories of Your miracles. Why aren't You acting now?" As human beings we long to live in a world that makes sense. Trauma turns that world upside down and leaves us struggling for equilibrium. We want answers when there are no answers. We want life to make sense again. We want someone or something to blame. We want God to act! We feel upended when He does not. We question if what we have believed is true.

One of my professors once said it this way: "We look at life and faith as if it were a mathematical formula: God's Law + our obedience = blessing." When that formula is turned upside down, human beings ask why. "Why did 9/11 happen? How could God have allowed the Holocaust? Why did the tornado kill my family?" are but a few of these questions. The author of Psalm 88 wrestles with these kinds of questions and begs God for action. What I want you to see right now is that he is not condemned for asking them.

Perhaps the reason he is not condemned is that there is a total honesty in his questions; no pretense; no false agenda—just a human being struggling with some of the deepest and most profound questions of life, just like you and me. They were personal questions: "God, when are you going to help *me*?!"

My experience was not one of trauma or tragedy, but those same questions took center place in my life for some time. My son was sinking into depression while I was assigned overseas. Three times I asked to be transferred back to the US. Three times I was told "NO!" in the way that only the US military can do. I prayed. I searched the Bible. I prayed harder. Then I read a book that advised to pray and have faith that God will answer. I remember reading something like this: "Pray, and believe that God will answer this week." I believed and prayed more intensely. I expected something would change that very week. Nothing!

We then made the painful decision to send the family back to the US on our own dime. A year and a half of separation ensued. We continued to pray and, you guessed it, still nothing happened. I began to think that my own faith was defective, that God did not hear me. And I must confess, I grew discouraged and began asking many of the same questions as the author of

Psalm 88 did. It seemed that God was constantly doing miracles in other people's lives, but not mine. I heard the stories of how He had miraculously worked in so many situations, but mine remained unchanged. Again, my pain was not related to a traumatic situation, but trauma magnifies these feelings and amplifies the intensity of such questions.

For many people, such questions feel off-limits, and most people don't ever get this honest with God. For some reason they perceive it as taboo, that God will strike them dead for even thinking such things. So, people tend to distance themselves from God and try their best to push any such questions far from their minds. We risk living in denial and at an artificially created distance from God.

Permission and Space

Healing often begins when a person feels as though he has permission to talk about his experiences—no matter how deep or dark they may be. People need space to wrestle with what has happened in their lives, to say what is really on their minds and in their hearts in the aftermath of trauma or loss without fear of further rejection. Psalm 88 provides a pattern in which we can find such healing.

In my job as both a hospital chaplain and military chaplain, I often sat with people as they described to me the traumas and losses they had endured. Simply being able to tell the story of what they have experienced—without someone appearing shocked or judgmental—is healing in and of itself. The young

Marine who served in Afghanistan, whom I described earlier, is an example. He told me all the ways in which his experiences had affected him and his relationships. He told me about his recurring nightmares, his drinking, and several other behaviors that were related to the trauma. At the end of our time together, nothing had changed in his life, but he thanked me for providing him a safe place to talk about things that he couldn't talk about anywhere else.

The writer of Psalm 88 provides us with a sample of what such permission and space look like. He talks about all his emotions—helplessness, desperation, feeling forgotten. He also throws out all his questions to God and pleads with Him, bargaining with God. He reminds God of all his losses and even accuses God: "Your fierce anger has overwhelmed me. Your terrors have paralyzed me" (v. 16 NLT). In essence, he is saying to God, *"You did this to me!"*

Does it surprise you that such language is in the Bible? Many people are completely blown away that this passage is actually in the text of the Bible. Their preconceived notions suggest that the Bible only talks about "should" and "ought" and doesn't give latitude to actually be a human being. Christians often do the same thing. They think that they should automatically be better equipped at dealing with difficulty or think that somehow it is unchristian to wrestle with difficulty and doubt.

The structure and language of Psalm 88 and its presence in the Bible should give those who feel as though they have no one and nowhere to share their deepest emotions permission to express the pent-up emotions of dealing with trauma.

Structure and Voice

The challenge is that when trauma hits, we seldom have the words to describe what we are feeling inside. Difficulty talking about our experiences inevitably leads to further isolation. So, it only makes sense that sometimes we need help with our words to express what we are feeling.

Trauma stunts creativity. The brain records traumatic memories differently than others. Sometimes there are no words to describe the experiences of trauma—only gut feelings. Phrases like, "forgotten from your care," "cut off," "Am I any good to you dead?" (see vv. 5, 10 NLT) can bring words to latent feelings that one struggles to understand and cannot articulate.

Similar to the experience I described earlier with the veteran's group, I also once read Psalm 88 to a group of military service members who had been diagnosed with PTSD. Afterward, I asked each of them to use the framework of this text to write their own lament. It was a very powerful experience. Hardened Marines and Navy SEALs found the language they needed to capture what had been going on inside for a long time. Some began to find healing in that moment. Some began expressing emotions in ways they had not previously. Others were able to express their anger at God as a result of that experience. There seems to be something powerful about a simple—but scary—act of speaking what we are feeling.

Act of Faith

Similar to the mother who tells her child, "Use your words," when the child is upset about something, the words of this psalm can be a kick start to beginning to understand and put into words the depths of our feelings in the aftermath of horrific trauma, loss, and grief of multiple and complex types.

Part of the reason for this is that it is easy to judge someone else's experience from the outside. It is easy to say that the questions that the psalmist asks are an anathema to the Christian faith, until they are *your* questions. Some well-meaning pastors have written that Christians should never be in the state of despair that is described in Psalm 88.

Take another look at the passage. Look at the intimacy that the author expresses to God. It is a difficult conversation for sure, as we have already mentioned. But don't miss this—notice it, please—it may be a bit obvious, but notice that the author is still talking to God! He does not understand anything that has happened to him; he feels as though he has been abandoned by everyone; he is questioning everything that he thought he believed about God; he is accusing God of inflicting this pain upon him; he tells God that the only friend he has left is the darkness as he sits alone with these thoughts—but he is still talking to God. In other words, he is attempting to maintain a relationship with God despite the obstacles.

On a daily basis therapists talk with people in conflict. Healthy resolution of conflict always means getting everything out on the table. Only when everyone's feelings are understood, validated, and accepted can the relationship begin to move forward. If that is how we deal with conflict in our relationships with other people, why do we feel that we cannot do the same with God? Do we think that somehow He cannot handle our feelings? That is absurd. He is the one who imagined and created human emotion in the first place. To think that the God who created the entire universe might be threatened by your emotions is like saying that a parent is threatened by the temper tantrums of a two-year-old.

If dealing with conflict in our human relationships means continuing to talk with one another, how much more so is this true with God? God desires to have a relationship with you. To have a relationship means that you must talk—even about hard things. While God is all-powerful, all-knowing, all-present, and makes no mistakes, we often don't understand and don't like what happens in life; we don't see all that God sees. When this happens, it feels like darkness is our closest friend. But God wants a relationship with you—which means talking with Him about all of the thoughts and feelings you have about everything in your life. Nothing is taboo or off-limits to Him; He can handle it even if it means that you are asking hard questions and telling Him about your most visceral emotions.

No Resolution

Those excruciating emotions often remain long after trauma is over. It seems as though there is nothing that can change them, because nothing can change the situation. It's sort of like watching a European movie that just ends. You know, the kind that leaves you saying, "What? That's the end?!" The kind that has no resolution.

If you look back at Psalm 88, that is exactly what we find. We find someone who has poured his heart out to God; who has asked the most difficult questions about life; who, as an act of faith, is still trying to talk with God and keep up the relationship. But that's it. The author is still sitting in the pit of whatever circumstances caused him to write this text in the first place. His only conclusion, "Darkness is my closest friend" (v. 18 NLT).

Sometimes that's just the way life and a relationship with God is. Tragedy strikes and we don't understand. We want to move on and get back to some type of normalcy in life. But that seems impossible. Loved ones are still dead; the memories of the rape are still there and will never go away; the fear left over after nearly drowning seems irrational, but you can never go near water without breaking into a sweat; the fear of getting caught in a riot again makes you panic anytime you go to a crowded Walmart; you still instinctively swerve on the freeway anytime you notice something that suspiciously reminds you of what an IED looked like in Iraq; you still avoid anyone or anything that may remind you of what you have been through. Some people try to bury their difficult emotions and pretend that they do not exist—pretend that what caused them does not exist—in a denial of emotions. Other people cover them up; they self-medicate with alcohol or drugs (both street drugs and abuse of prescription medications like opioid pain medications). Still others turn to illicit relationships, like having an affair, engaging in the "hookup" culture, prostitution, or porn. They are longing to have a relationship that will fill the pain and emptiness they feel inside.

Ultimately, none of this helps. Even worse, reactions like avoidance and self-medicating only push people further from the healing they are seeking. Sometimes the only way to move forward is to sit still. The only way out of "the pit" is to sit in the pit for a while, to stay there long enough that you begin to accept the new realities of your life without trying to change them. Only then, after enough time has passed, can you look back and say, "That was the pit I was in."

How long does this go on? Only you will know. For example, in the 1990s romantic comedy *Sleepless in Seattle*, Tom Hanks's character describes to a radio psychiatrist what it was like to lose his wife. He says, "At first I had to remind myself to breathe in and out. Then after a while, I didn't have to remind myself to breathe in and out." For some it takes a lifetime. One Vietnam veteran did not begin to deal with his combat experience until forty years later, when he finally retired. He had been a workaholic and kept himself so busy that he did not have to think about Vietnam. When he finally retired, he had nothing to occupy his time and finally allowed himself to begin thinking about the pit he was in.

If you are going through a period of grief, trauma, or loss, perhaps the place that your healing needs to begin is to get comfortable with the statement of the psalmist, "Darkness is my closest friend" (v. 18 NLT). Right now, there is nothing else for you to do than to simply begin to make friends with the darkness in which you find yourself.

Guided Reflection

Have your life experiences left you feeling as though darkness is your closest friend? Have you tried to make friends with that darkness in the past and failed? Use the following ideas while you find yourself in that pit of darkness:

1. Find a quiet place and read Psalm 88 again. As you do so, notice the raw emotion within the text. Then notice your own raw emotions that are touched as you read. For example, are there words that you noticed that make you feel angry, forgotten, or abandoned? Acknowledge those feelings. Don't label them as good or bad. Just begin to *notice* what you are feeling without judgment. As you notice your emotions, give yourself permission to *feel* how you feel (to be angry, if you are angry, etc.).

2. Get a blank notebook and use the words of Psalm 88 to write your own lament. Use its words to get you started if you feel stuck. But keep writing until you feel as though you have "hit bottom," or "spoken," as much as you feel you can.

3. Give yourself permission to ask God the hard questions, the ones that are on your mind that you have not dared to speak to anyone else. Write them down. Ask them out loud. Whatever

it takes, just get the questions out in the open, even if just for yourself.

The theme of these exercises is to keep talking with God. He wants a relationship with you; keep your end of the relationship open. Don't try to escape prematurely from the pain in which you find yourself. Begin now, every day, to do your best to accept whatever new reality in which you find yourself.

Chapter 2

Where Are You?

> *"My God, my God, why have
> you abandoned me?"*
> Psalm 22:1a NLT

PICTURE THIS. YOU ARE WATCHING an action movie. Soldiers have been covertly dropped into a location where they are not supposed to be, to perform a top-secret mission. They have all the support they need, until someone thousands of miles away gets cold feet and, because of political pressure, cancels the mission. Rather than pull the clandestine team out, they are simply left, with all communication and support resources withdrawn. As the team is overrun, radio calls can be heard saying, "We need air support, where the #%!# are you!?" While the audience is appalled at what has happened, they know the whole story. The team, however, is simply left to suffer alone.[2]

That is how trauma often feels; it seems as though someone should be able to give a reason for what has happened. But those who experience sudden and traumatic loss feel alone. They are left wondering what just happened to them and how on earth their lives are ever going to be the same. Traumatic events can trigger PTSD and leave a person to suffer a multitude of symptoms in which they reexperience the trauma. They can also cause moral injury, where a person wrestles with whether they could have done something to prevent the trauma, or worse, wonder if they did something that somehow caused it.

Trauma creates desperation—the kind of desperation that can be heard in a mother's voice when her child is missing; it is in the sound of a soldier's yell under fire; it is found in private emergency room waiting areas reserved for those receiving the worst news of their lives. Desperation creates the questions that some dare not ask, and the questions that eat away at their heart and soul when left undealt with. They are the questions of a human being to his creator: "God, where are You! Why has this horrific loss occurred? If You are all-powerful, then why did this happen to me? If You are all-loving, don't You care how bad this hurts?" Such questions are part of the universal human experience. They are questions that plague us deep in our souls; questions that scream out and beg for an answer. At a gut level, we just want to yell, "God, *why*?" We plead for answers and have no space for people who won't be real with us. We long for someone who can relate, someone who can give us perspective on what we are going through in the darkest hours of our lives.

Throughout human history, people have wrestled with questions like these. Philosophers and theologians have debated them along with the meaning of suffering and life itself. Ancient Israel's King David, known for writing poetry, penned the words of Psalm 22. He knew what it was like to be hunted and on the run, to wonder why God seemed to allow evil to prosper in the world. This passage captures the volatility of David's emotions as he wrestled with such questions. Listen to the emotions present and notice the radical honesty in these words. Look for glimpses of hopefulness, asking: *Where have I heard this before?* Finally, ask: *How does this provide perspective for what I am going through?*

> My God, my God, why have you abandoned me?
> Why are you so far away when I groan for help?
> Every day I call to you, my God, but you do not answer.
> Every night I lift my voice, but I find no relief.
>
> Yet you are holy,
> enthroned on the praises of Israel.
> Our ancestors trusted in you,
> and you rescued them.
> They cried out to you and were saved.
> They trusted in you and were never disgraced.
>
> But I am a worm and not a man.
> I am scorned and despised by all!
> Everyone who sees me mocks me.
> They sneer and shake their heads, saying,
> "Is this the one who relies on the LORD?
> Then let the LORD save him!

WHERE ARE YOU?

If the LORD loves him so much,
    let the LORD rescue him!"

Yet you brought me safely from my mother's
    womb
    and led me to trust you at my mother's
    breast.
I was thrust into your arms at my birth.
    You have been my God from the moment
    I was born.

Do not stay so far from me,
    for trouble is near,
    and no one else can help me.
My enemies surround me like a herd of bulls;
    fierce bulls of Bashan have hemmed me in!
Like lions they open their jaws against me,
    roaring and tearing into their prey.
My life is poured out like water,
    and all my bones are out of joint.
My heart is like wax,
    melting within me.
My strength has dried up like sunbaked clay.
    My tongue sticks to the roof of my mouth.
    You have laid me in the dust and left me
    for dead.
My enemies surround me like a pack of dogs;
    an evil gang closes in on me.
    They have pierced my hands and feet.

I can count all my bones.
> My enemies stare at me and gloat.
They divide my garments among themselves
> and throw dice for my clothing.

O Lord, do not stay far away!
> You are my strength; come quickly to my aid!
Save me from the sword;
> spare my precious life from these dogs.
Snatch me from the lion's jaws
> and from the horns of these wild oxen.
> (vv. 1–21 NLT)

Universal Human Experience

Human beings have suffered through war, disease, abuse, and natural disaster since the beginning of time. As a result, questions like those above have been part of human existence since the beginning of recorded history. Hebrew wisdom literature, Greek philosophers, and early Christian theologians have all attempted to resolve the problem of evil, pain, and suffering in our world. But the fact of the matter is that such questions just hurt. If we are honest with ourselves, we have all experienced the bewilderment of such pain in our world in one way or another. Nearly everyone I have ever met asks some version of these questions when tragedy strikes: "God, why did this happen? God, where are You?" In fact, people have often said to me, "It feels like God is not there," as they deal with the aftermath of trauma and traumatic loss. In such times, human beings struggle to gain our equilibrium. But the inevitable question that most people have, the one that has plagued humanity throughout its existence is: "How could this have happened if there really is a God who loves me and is as powerful as He claims to be?" So, if you have ever struggled with questions like these, welcome to the human race. You are not alone. The question of why bad things happen is nearly always the first thing that comes out of the mouths of those who experience trauma, and it is almost always directed toward God.

- God, why did the tornado take out my house and my family, and the neighbors were spared?
- God, why did my buddy get blown up by a car bomb, but I seemed to make it without a scratch?
- God, why did my son get shot by a random bullet on his way to work?
- God, why did he pick me as the one to attack and rape?

Notice how King David phrases these questions. He demands: "My God, my God, why have you abandoned me? Why are you so far away when I groan for help? Every day I call to you, my God, but you do not answer. Every night I lift my voice, but I find no relief" (vv. 1–2 NLT). David describes feelings of abandonment and isolation. He finds no answers and no relief in his searching, and he wonders aloud why God feels so distant. We see that his emotions are raw; he groans for help. David's questions are our questions; his emotions are our emotions.

People tend to react to such emotional questions in the aftermath of trauma in one of several ways. First, some people say, like David, "I find no relief." But they go one step further and say something like, "There are no answers to my questions, so what use is religion? If there is a God, how could He allow all of this to happen? I cannot believe in God." Consider the following: An atheist who lost a family member once told me that he would like to understand more about God's love. Yet, inevitably, our conversations about God and His love always ended up at the same place. He would say, "No! I just cannot believe in a god who allows innocent children to suffer abuse and neglect, who allows so many people around the world to starve and suffer without enough food, or who allows wars and things like COVID-19 and so many other diseases." For him, the feelings David expresses are proof positive that God could not exist.

For others, the questions seem to be too much. Like David, their questions are not answered, and they find difficulty in the constant groaning of their emotional state. So instead, they prefer not to think about their pain. They focus on distracting themselves so that they don't have to think about their trauma. For example, one young veteran of the war in Afghanistan focused on life with his girlfriend and partying with friends. For a time, he was successful in not thinking about all he had been through. He was in denial. Eventually, his experiences forced their way out, as often happens when a person is in denial, and he was hospitalized in a psychiatric facility that could care for the symptoms of PTSD that he was experiencing.

Similarly, still others respond with what I call a "but God" mentality. They also cannot find answers to their questions, so they stop asking them. They too quickly move from the hurt and pain of the trauma, to saying, "But God is good, and I trust Him." While it is important to continue to trust God in the aftermath of trauma, some people can deny their own emotions in the process. This denial of very real human emotions, feelings that David freely expresses, often leads to religious and psychological dysfunction. (More will be said in chapter 6 about deliberately choosing to trust God.)

Finally, some people think that their emotional reactions to the grief of a traumatic experience represent a problem. This is actually very common in the Western world, where culture places extreme value on happiness and positive emotions. Trauma survivors don't like how their emotions make them feel, so they tend to think that something is wrong because they are having normal emotional responses. Yet David freely expresses these more difficult emotions. He lets them out and engages with both the feelings and their sources. Modern culture should follow the example of his ancient wisdom.

Maybe part of the problem is that you have been taught not to question God. You think that somehow these questions are inappropriate, or even wrong, to ask. Yet if we are honest with ourselves, we have all had these questions at some point in our lives. The questions may be buried deeply somewhere in your psyche, somewhere that you don't like to go, but they are there nonetheless. To be human is to experience pain and suffering. But it is also normal for humans to have emotional responses and to ask these types of questions. Some people bury the questions; others shout them defiantly. In order to find healing in the aftermath of whatever traumatic loss has visited your life, you must acknowledge your humanity and give yourself permission to let the questions out, for to have such questions is to be human.

Pleas to Answer

Psalm 22 doesn't just deal with questions. David begs God to answer! Notice what he says:

> Do not stay so far from me,
> > for trouble is near,
> > and no one else can help me.
>
> O LORD, do not stay far away!
> > You are my strength; come quickly to my aid!
>
> Save me from the sword;
> > spare my precious life from these dogs.
>
> Snatch me from the lion's jaws
> > and from the horns of these wild oxen.
>
> (vv. 11, 19–21 NLT)

You can feel his pain at a gut level. He begs God to not remain distant but, instead, to help him. He even says that God is the *only* one who can help. His prayers are intense pleas filled with expectation—expectation that God will hear and answer. In times of tragedy, we scream for God to do something, to change the horrific situation at hand. Bargaining is one of the commonly accepted stages of grief. Like David, we want God to do something to change the situation; to bring back a loved one who has died; to turn back time to the day before the terrorist attack or natural disaster; to do something that only God can do.

People instinctively know that God is the only one who can answer; they plead with Him to do so, regardless of their belief system. Recently I read an article recounting research into the number of atheists who admitted that they prayed, particularly at times of grief and loss. While it makes no sense intellectually that an atheist would pray to a God in whom he or she does not believe, it makes complete sense emotionally. One popular sitcom features just such a story.[3] A father is taken to the emergency room as he is experiencing chest pain. His children join him after a few hours. The youngest, a child prodigy who does not believe in God, wanders into the chapel. The voice-over says that, in that moment, he needed one of his academic heroes, who believed in God, to be right. Emotionally, he needed God to be real and to intervene, even though, intellectually, he could not bring himself to believe.

Human beings long for God to answer when they are hurting and powerless to change their circumstances. We want to know that God is there and can do something about our pain. Just like David, we cry out and beg God to hear and answer our suffering. Yet God does not always answer, leaving us hurting and confused.

One Who Can Relate

Not only is suffering part of the universal human condition, but our questions about our pain are also completely normal and part of the human experience as well. We don't just have theoretical questions though; we want someone to do something about them. We want God to answer, but there is more. People have a deep need to be understood, to have their feelings validated. We want to know that someone understands us. Human beings need to know that someone can relate to our suffering. Perhaps some of the words that David expressed seem familiar. Eyewitnesses of the last words of Jesus Christ as He hung on the cross during His crucifixion recorded that Jesus quoted the first line of Psalm 22: "My God, my God, why have you abandoned me?" (Matt. 27:46; Mark 15:34 NLT). Perhaps it is more familiar in some other translations of the original Greek New Testament text: "My God, My God, why have you forsaken me?"[4]

Volumes have been written about the theological significance of this statement. But before launching into yet another, can I just say that maybe Jesus said this because He was human? Certainly, He is both divine and human; the fact of the matter is that He *IS* both God and man. As a human being, He hurt the same way we hurt. He felt the gravity of humanity's physical, emotional, psychological, and spiritual pain. He experienced each of those types of pain as He hung suspended between life and death. He can relate to your pain because He experienced it Himself. As He shouted these words from the cross, "My God, my God, why have you abandoned me?" (Matt. 27:46;

Mark 15:34 NLT), He was experiencing the most painful and cruel form of public execution the world has ever devised. It involved nails through the hands and feet, and the victim hung on those nails in a manner that slowly suffocated them.

It was a humiliating experience as well. Roman crucifixion stripped people naked before crucifying them. I know, artist renderings and crucifixes picture Jesus wearing a loin cloth, but that was not the reality. In addition, these executions were performed along the main public thoroughfare as people entered and exited the city. A list of crimes was posted over the executees, heads as a public spectacle and to send a clear message: Don't mess with Rome! In Jesus's case, He had been awake all night the previous night praying so intensely that there might be another way, that He literally sweated blood—only to find Himself on the cross anyway. Furthermore, Jesus was alone. His followers deserted Him when the Roman soldiers arrested Him. Physical pain, emotional anguish, spiritual silence, fatigue, isolation—can you relate? People often describe these things during and after their traumatic event.

Jesus Christ experienced what you have experienced. He knows what physical pain is like, to be suddenly and brutally executed, and He can relate to your most embarrassing situations. He understands what it is like to pray intensely for something, only to have the answer be, "No." He also knows what it is like to be abandoned by friends when things get tough.

Perhaps you can't bring yourself to say that you feel abandoned by God. There could be many reasons for this. You may have been taught that it is not appropriate to doubt God, and saying out loud that you feel that He has abandoned you would seem as though you are doing so. If that is the case, think about it this way: What we witness as Jesus quotes the first line of Psalm 22 is God the Son saying to God the Father, with His emotions at their most raw and vulnerable state, "Why have you abandoned me?" (Matt. 27:46; Mark 15:34 NLT). If it is okay for Jesus, the divine/human, God/Man, Son of God to say this to God the Father, maybe, just maybe, it is okay for you and me to do the same. As you reflect on that thought, may I ask: How does it feel to know that Jesus can relate to such feelings?

Over the years, as I have encountered countless military service members, veterans, hospital patients, and rape victims, I have always been amazed at the healing power of a shared experience. For example, several years ago, a group of Iraqi war veterans gathered in a coffee shop to talk about their experiences of what it was like to come home from Iraq. They talked about things like their startle reflexes around loud noises, anxiety around large crowds, and vigilance when they noticed any trash along the roadside that might look like an IED. As the night ended and they began to part ways, they all said to one another, "Tonight, I realized that it is not just me. Other people know what I have been through. I'm not crazy." Sharing experiences with another provided them with the realization that others could relate. As a result, they increasingly gave themselves permission to be real with one another and found healing as they did. Human beings naturally draw comfort from one another through shared trauma and shared experience.

If support groups like the one just mentioned can make such a difference for veterans and survivors of traumatic events, perhaps knowing that Jesus also experienced feelings of abandonment by God will help you to be honest with God and allow yourself to ask questions that you may have kept bottled up until now.

Perspective

When we are experiencing times in life where we feel as though we have been abandoned by God, it can also help to catch a glimpse of the larger perspective. The words that David wrote in Psalm 22 were penned somewhere around 1,000 BC. Yet as Jesus quotes the first line of the passage, many of the things it goes on to describe in detail were happening to Him, in those very moments, a thousand years later. Notice in the passages that follow what is written in Psalm 22, circa 1,000 BC, and then notice each of the passages describing in detail what Jesus experienced.

Mocking

But I am a worm and not a man. I am scorned and despised by all! Everyone who sees me mocks me. They sneer and shake their heads, saying, "Is this the one who relies on the LORD? Then let the LORD save him! If the LORD loves him so much, let the LORD rescue him!" (Ps. 22:6–8 NLT)

They put a purple robe on him, then twisted together a crown of thorns and set it on him. And they began to call out to him, "Hail, king of the Jews!" Again and again they struck him on the head with a staff and spit on him. Falling on their knees, they paid homage to him. And when they had mocked him, they took off the purple robe and put his own clothes on him. . . .

Those who passed by hurled insults at him, shaking their heads and saying, "So! You who are going to destroy the temple and build it in three days, come down from the cross and save yourself!" In the same way the chief priests and the teachers of the law mocked him among themselves. "He saved others," they said, "but he can't save himself! Let this Messiah, this king of Israel, come down now from the cross, that we may see and believe." Those crucified with him also heaped insults on him. (Mark 15:17–20a, 29–32 NIV)

Crucifixion

They have pierced my hands and feet. (Ps. 22:16b NLT)

When they came to the place called the Skull, they crucified him there, along with the criminals—one on his right, the other on his left. (Luke 23:33 NIV)

Thirst

My tongue sticks to the roof of my mouth. (Ps. 22:15b NLT)

Later, knowing that everything had now been finished, and so that Scripture would be fulfilled, Jesus said, "I am thirsty." A jar of wine vinegar was there, so they soaked a sponge in it, put the sponge on a stalk of the hyssop plant, and lifted it to Jesus' lips. (John 19:28–29 NIV)

Gambling for His Clothing

They divide my garments among themselves and throw dice for my clothing. (Ps. 22:18 NLT)

When the soldiers crucified Jesus, they took his clothes and divided them into four parts, a part for each soldier. They also took the tunic, which was seamless, woven in one piece from the top. So they said to one another, "Let's not tear it, but cast lots for it, to see who gets it." (John 19:23–24a)

No Broken Bones

I can count all my bones. (Ps. 22:17a NLT)

The soldiers therefore came and broke the legs of the first man who had been crucified with Jesus, and then those of the other. But when they came to Jesus and found that he was already dead, they did not break his legs. Instead, one of the soldiers pierced Jesus' side with a spear, bringing a sudden flow of blood and water. The man who saw it has given testimony, and his testimony is true. He knows that he tells the truth, and he testifies so that you also may believe. These things happened so that the scripture would be fulfilled: "Not one of his bones will be broken," and, as another scripture says, "They will look on the one they have pierced." (John 19:32–37 NIV)

These are but a few of the parallels; one could go further in making comparisons. But notice the incredible level of detail that is described and would unfold a thousand years later. Take in the gravity of that for a moment. God knew every detail of what Christ would suffer on the cross a thousand years before it happened. It is but one reminder that God is outside of time and space. He can see the events of our lives from beginning to end. He knew a thousand years before Christ's crucifixion the exact manner in which it would take place, including the level of detail described in the passages above. In the same way, God understands your current suffering as well. He knows about it now, and He knew about it thousands of years ago. How does it feel to realize that God knew the exact details of your current situation millennia ago? Gaining God's perspective, perspective that He knows the details of your life and He knew what you would be going through right now, millennia ago, may give you the strength you need to get through another day of dealing with your traumatic loss.

Perspective makes a difference. Early in my career as a Navy chaplain, I spent five years assigned to naval aviation units. I love airplanes and all things about flying, so it was a dream come true. As you might imagine, I learned a lot about aviation during that time. One thing of particular importance that I discovered during all those hours in-flight, on the flight line, and in simulators was that pilots are taught to trust their instruments. Failure to do so is often deadly.

Several years later, I was on a commercial airliner connecting through San Francisco International Airport, on my way to Japan. As is often the case, the Bay Area was engulfed in thick fog and visibility outside the airplane was nonexistent. As the plane made a right turn to line up with the runway for final approach, I leaned back in my chair, reflecting on the details that I was confident the pilots were watching on the flight deck, things like altimeter, heading, air speed, rate of descent, angle of approach, air traffic control frequencies, and a host of other details. In short, I completely trusted them to get me on the ground because their instruments allowed them to see the unseen and guide the plane safely to the runway.

Suddenly, another thought occurred. The previous night, my mother-in-law had read a devotional thought someone had written to our family. We were in limbo, on the doorstep of eighteen months of separation as I prepared to return to Japan to complete my tour of duty there, and my wife and kids remained behind in the States. As I mentioned in chapter one, we had all prayed that it would not come to this, but it had. We were confused and bewildered. As my mother-in-law read, the refrain of the devotional was of the individual saying to Jesus, "I trust You." Quite frankly, I was irritated as she read it. I had trusted Jesus, but He had not answered—at least not the way I wanted. As the plane descended in the San Francisco fog, I remembered the refrain—the soft, "I trust You." Then it hit me! If I could calmly trust pilots, whom I did not know, to get me safely on the ground because they could see what I could not through their instruments, why could I not trust my unknown and uncertain future to a God whom I had known and worshiped since I was a child?

Just like the audience in the movie described at the beginning of the chapter knows what has happened, while the soldiers who have been abandoned have no idea, so it is with faith in God. God sees through the fog—He sees the entirety of the story in moments when we cannot—and simply asks us to trust Him in the same way and to a deeper level than we trust pilots to get us on the ground when we are flying through dense clouds.

The Jewish prophet Isaiah said it this way, "LORD, you are my God; I will exalt you and praise your name, *for in perfect faithfulness you have done wonderful things, things planned long ago*" (Isa. 25:1 NIV, emphasis added). That is exactly what Jesus experienced as He hung on the cross and cried out to God, "My God, my God, why have you abandoned me? . . ." (Matt. 27:46; Mark 15:34 NLT), even as the very fulfillment of what had been written about Him long ago was occurring in those very moments.

While perspective helps, the opposite is true as well. It is extremely difficult to live through those times when the only thing that you can see is the suffering before you. Time and time again, Navy recruits in the earliest stages of their training would say to me, "Sir, I think I made a mistake joining the Navy. I don't think I can do this." Because of the difficulty of the boot camp experience and the lack of perspective about what the training experience was designed to do, many initially simply wanted the stress and physical demands to end. Yet what most discovered as the weeks wore on was that there was purpose in their adversity, they were not as alone as they initially imagined, and they were able to accomplish more than they initially believed about themselves.

When trauma and tragedy strike, we often feel abandoned by God and others. We struggle to see any purpose in what we are experiencing, and the pain is so intense that it leaves us wondering whether we can deal with it. Just like Jesus, we cry out in our humanity and ask God, "Why have you abandoned me?"

Guided Reflection

Feelings of being abandoned by God are part of the universal human experience. Being human means living in the uncomfortable space of being separated from God, and we wrestle with the difficulty of such feelings. We try to make sense out of what is unexplainable: the problem of human suffering. We plead with God to answer; we beg Him to intercede. But we often stop short of actually saying to Him, "You abandoned me!" We do this for many reasons, mostly because we fear going where angels fear to tread. Yet Jesus Himself expresses our pain and His. He says to God the Father what we all want to say: "Why have you abandoned me?" (Matt. 27:46; Mark 15:34 NLT). Then gradually God allows us perspective on our suffering, perspective that He knew thousands of years ago what would be happening in our lives right now. That glimmer of perspective can then help us begin to recognize that perhaps He has not abandoned us altogether, that maybe He is trustworthy after all.

As you reflect over this chapter, reread Psalm 22. Ask yourself which of the following is most meaningful to you:

- Human suffering and questions about why it happens are part of being human. If you are experiencing this, you are normal. Welcome to the human race!
- It is okay to express feelings of abandonment by God *to* God. Jesus did it, so it must be okay.

- God sees through the fog that you are experiencing in your life right now. He has an eternal perspective on your suffering.

Now ask yourself: Why does this resonate so much with me? Who can I share my insights with? Take time to write down your replies to these questions.

Chapter 3

Safe Space

*"Refuge: A condition of being safe or sheltered
from pursuit, danger, or trouble."*
Oxford Dictionary

FIFTY-SIX DEGREES SOUTH LATITUDE; 67 degrees west longitude; 70 knots of wind over deck; sea state 11 (forty-foot swells with white water over the flight deck). Such were the conditions on Sunday morning when, aboard the aircraft carrier *USS Nimitz*, we rounded Cape Horn at the tip of South America, moving from Atlantic to Pacific, through some of the roughest seas in the world.

The morning began somewhat normally. I was preparing to lead Sunday worship, but the seas were not cooperating. Soon, I would be confined to my rack, so seasick I could barely function. I prayed for death, the Rapture, or a sudden and miraculous calming of the seas. But no relief came. I thought about my first time at sea, in much milder conditions—only five- to ten-foot seas—aboard the amphibious ship *USS Mount Vernon*. After those ten days at sea, I had gotten used to walking on the edge of the bulkhead, bracing myself when the deck and bulkhead seemed to be at a forty-five-degree angle. This was different. Everything within me screamed to escape. But there was no way to do so. The only way to get through this was to suffer it out like everyone else. So I ate saltine crackers, took as much meclizine as was safe, did what little work I could, and continued to pray for calm seas. After three days, conditions began to return to normal as we made our way up the Chilean coast. But the experience was unnerving.

Such unsettled feelings often accompany grief, trauma, and loss. It feels as though the ground underneath us has turned into mush and all we thought as solid throughout our lives now is uncertain, transient, and unstable. One particular sailor who had just shared the details of a life-changing situation described feeling as though the rug had been ripped out from underneath her. What a great visual picture! Imagine that you are standing in the middle of a room on a large area rug when, suddenly and with great force, the rug is ripped from below your feet. You lose your balance, hit the floor, maybe roll for a way, and then stagger to get up, find your bearings, and figure out what just happened. Traumatic loss does just that. It leaves us wondering what just happened and feeling as though nothing is stable, just like being on a ship in a rough sea. In the aftermath of such life-altering events, we humans simply want to find some source of stability—something to hold on to—and catch our breath as we seek to regain our equilibrium and figure out our next move. It's as if we were hanging on to the jagged rocks of a seashore, desperately searching for safety.

The writer of ancient Israel's Psalm 46 spoke of such safety. The message of this passage inspired Martin Luther to write the reformation hymn, "A Mighty Fortress Is Our God." Psalm 46 gives some insight into God's protection and provision of humanity in our most desperate situations:

> God is our refuge and strength,
> > an ever-present help in trouble.
> Therefore we will not fear, though the earth
> > give way
> > and the mountains fall into the heart of
> > the sea,
> though its waters roar and foam
> > and the mountains quake with their
> > surging.
>
> There is a river whose streams make glad the
> > city of God,
> > the holy place where the Most High
> > dwells.
> God is within her, she will not fall;
> > God will help her at break of day.
> Nations are in uproar, kingdoms fall;
> > he lifts his voice, the earth melts.
>
> The LORD Almighty is with us;
> > the God of Jacob is our fortress.
>
> Come and see what the LORD has done,
> > the desolations he has brought on the
> > earth.

> He makes wars cease
>> to the ends of the earth.
> He breaks the bow and shatters the spear;
>> he burns the shields with fire.
> He says, "Be still, and know that I am God;
>> I will be exalted among the nations,
>> I will be exalted in the earth."
>
> The LORD Almighty is with us;
>> the God of Jacob is our fortress. (NIV)

What we are really looking for in the aftermath of trauma, grief, and loss is to simply find a safe space. Safety and security are among our primary needs in dealing with all that we have experienced. A safe space may literally be a place where you can find physical safety. But a safe space also means a place where you can talk freely and be yourself. Counselors and therapists work to create emotional safety for their clients in order to foster an environment of care and healing.

What Terrifies Us

Just as it is unnerving to be aboard a ship in rough seas, there are many things in life that cause human beings absolute terror. Most often, these are the sources of trauma and traumatic loss that we experience in life. Consider the stories of tornado survivors who often describe the experience as hearing a jet engine or a freight train coming toward them, or the experience of someone who has just survived a car accident, and as though he is still trying to sort out what happened, says, "The other car just came out of nowhere. There was nothing I could do." Combat veterans know the fear related to the sudden burst of enemy fire, the sound of incoming artillery or mortar fire, and the explosion of an IED. Trauma and emergency room nurses and physicians know the sights and smells of trying to save a person with life-threatening injuries. Assault victims know the horror and "pure evil" of another person who overpowers and abuses them physically or sexually. In short, our world is filled with terror in many different forms and on many different levels.

Such has been the case throughout human history. Not since before Adam and Eve tasted the forbidden fruit of the garden of Eden has humanity known what it is like to truly live in peace and serenity—with the absence of war, terror, natural disaster, and all the other forms of violence we know in our world.

Many of the things that cause us worry and fear today are like those that the writer of Psalm 46 (NIV) describes:

- ". . . though the earth give way and the mountains fall into the heart of the sea, though its waters roar and foam and the mountains quake with their surging." (vv. 2b–3)
- "Nations are in uproar, kingdoms fall . . ." (v. 6a)

Those passages remind me of the dramatic videos that are sometimes captured of glaciers in Alaska or other places as they calve, when part of the glacier breaks off into the ocean. Such recordings are awe-inspiring, from a distance. As tons of ice suddenly fall into the sea, the waves created can be more than twenty feet tall. Small boats are easily swamped and nearby beaches are flooded.

What the writer of Psalm 46 (NIV) is describing is something similar: the mountains themselves falling into the heart of the sea—a terrifying event. Each year we hear stories from around the world about rockslides or mudslides that take the lives of many and leave others fearful. Beyond rockslides, the writer also describes events that we may know as tidal waves, hurricanes, and other major storms: "its [the sea's] waters roar and foam" (v. 3a). He continues: ". . . and the mountains quake with their surging" (v. 3b), which could refer to earthquakes or simply the power of the ocean violently crashing into a rocky shore. Either way, the imagery is of cataclysmic events that make us feel small and helpless. In my mind, I see a person desperately holding on to a rocky cliff, with large waves crashing below and no way of escape.

Later in the passage, the writer describes another horrifying set of circumstances: "Nations are in uproar, kingdoms fall. . . ." (v. 6a). World events like coups, insurrections, invasions, ultimatums, and all-out war each strike fear and uncertainty into our hearts. We watch the news and worry about the impact of such events on our lives. Events like these strike terror into the human heart. They unnerve us. They cause us to question what is safe and how to trust all that we think we know. For example, one spring day in Fallujah, Iraq, two young Marines were running toward me, and I could see the fear in their eyes. They stopped momentarily to warn me that incoming mortar fire had hit a hundred yards away. Gasping to catch their breath, they described how they had narrowly escaped.

Let's face it. The world can be a terrifying place. The power of nature makes us feel small and afraid when disasters hit. Warfare strikes fear into the heart of the most battle-hardened. But the loss of a loved one to cancer can be equally scary. Grief, trauma, and loss interrupt our lives and cause us to look for something stable. The mental health crisis is a reminder that human beings are scared—that we simply want to find an oasis of rest, hope, and peace in a world filled with death, destruction, uncertainty, chaos, and loneliness. We, indeed, need a safe space.

Refuge

But notice what Psalm 46 (NIV) says about such an oasis: "God is our refuge and strength, an ever-present help in trouble" (v. 1). The oasis of refuge that is described here is not a place, but a person—God Himself. The writer then says, "Therefore we will not fear . . ." (v. 2), as he goes on to describe all the calamities that were mentioned in the past few paragraphs. Then, there is this refrain that repeats: "The LORD Almighty is with us; the God of Jacob is our fortress" (vv. 7, 11).

The message of this passage is that God is not only with us, but He is also our refuge and place of safety when our world is falling apart. Whether mountains are falling into the heart of the sea, or geopolitical events occur where "nations are in uproar" (v. 6), God is there. He is our refuge in the middle of such chaos.

So, what does it mean to be a refuge? As hinted in the chapter title, the *Oxford Dictionary* defines refuge as: "A condition of being safe or sheltered from pursuit, danger, or trouble."[5] Sometimes a shelter is a place to escape a storm. At other times, it is an area of sanctuary. But it can also be a lifeline that provides safety.

When I was twelve years old, my family, along with another from our church, went into the mountains of Southern Oregon on a beautiful Saturday afternoon to cut firewood for the winter. As was often the case on such trips, when we arrived, all the kids explored the woods. The rule was that we had to stay close enough that we could still hear the chain saws running as our parents cut wood. When the saws stopped, we were to start making our way back. On this occasion, they were cutting wood near an old, abandoned uranium mine. It was an open pit that had filled with water and formed a small lake.

Around the lake were three roads that had been cut into the surrounding mountainside as the pit had been cut from the earth. Each of the three roads was higher up on the side of the pit. So my sisters and I, and the three boys and one girl from the other family, charged off on our adventure, choosing, of course, the most difficult route of the third and highest road. Our plan was to walk all the way around the pit, and from the highest road we would be able to easily crest the hill that would take us back to where our parents were working.

The plan was going well and we were enjoying our adventure, kicking rocks and pine cones, and breaking sticks. Then, when we were about two-thirds of the way around, we discovered that the road ended before us. Rather than returning the long way, the way we had come, we chose to forge on. The path was difficult. We were walking on a steep incline, in loose rock, but it all seemed well. That is, until the loose rock under my feet gave way, and I found myself sliding down the steep incline toward a cliff that dropped more than a hundred feet into waters below. There was nothing I could do—nothing to grab onto! I was going to go over the ledge. It was like trying to swim in loose rock.

Then, just as my legs and torso went over the edge, I grabbed a small branch that was growing out of the edge of the cliff. Slowly, I pulled myself up and carefully made it back to the group. My sister was crying, saying that she thought I was going to die, and my friends were shaken. We immediately returned to our parents. But the moment I grabbed that branch, I knew instinctively that God had placed it there; that He had allowed it to be in exactly the right place at the right time to save my life. God was my refuge and strength that day as I hung on for dear life.

There is nothing quite like the most traumatic events in our lives that make us feel unsafe. Yet, the writer of Psalm 46 (NIV) affirms that "God is our refuge and strength" (v. 1a), and he goes on to add that God is "an ever-present help in trouble" (v. 1b). Just like the branch I caught at twelve years old, God is always there in the darkest times of your life. That branch was God's refuge and strength in the most terrifying moment of my young life. The branch also saved my life. That does not always happen. Traumatic events still happen. But look carefully back at the passage one more time. It reads: "God is . . . an ever-present help *in* trouble" (v. 1, emphasis added). God does not look at our difficulties from the distance. Nor does He wait until things settle down to come near and encourage us. He is there with us in the middle of the most difficult and painful moments of life.

No Fear

Because God's presence is indeed with us, the writer of Psalm 46 (NIV) concludes: "Therefore we will not fear" (v. 2). Trauma induces fear. As indicated earlier in the chapter, the world is full of things that cause human beings absolute terror; things that cause us to cling to something that helps us to feel safe. Yet the writer of the psalm says that because "God is our refuge and strength, an ever-present help in trouble . . . we will not fear" (vv. 1–2). It seems a bit counterintuitive that we could be so calm when everything in the world is falling apart around us. I'm not sure about you, but if the mountains started falling into the ocean, I would probably be a bit afraid. I was twelve years old when Mount St. Helens erupted, sending volcanic ash thousands of feet into the air and liquefying glaciers and dirt into giant, fast-moving mudslides. The story dominated the news not just in the Pacific Northwest, but around the country.

It is in just such chaotic environments that Psalm 46 says that we will not fear. It is not because the situations we face in life are not fearful and scare us to death—quite the opposite. As mentioned already, there is plenty in the world that frightens us. Instead, it is because God is with us—that He is our refuge and strength—that we are able to keep fear at bay.

This "no fear" mentality is not something dreamed up by clever marketers, nor is it something mustered by adrenaline junkies. It is supernatural! God supernaturally gives us peace when peace is the last thing we should be experiencing in the midst of chaos, trauma, grief, and loss. To this day, I cannot explain it, but when those two Marines came running toward me in Fallujah, and I heard the subsequent alarms indicating incoming fire, I was completely calm. My heart rate was not elevated, nor was there any sense of panic in my mind or body. I simply walked to the closest shelter. When I arrived, the people there looked at me like I was crazy or clueless (either of which, I suppose, could have been true). But the reality is that God produced in me a peace that was well beyond my own ability to express strength or courage, because I am by nature an anxious person. Faith in God provides peace in our lives when all around, the world is falling apart.

Fear is a normal and natural reaction to life-threatening and non-life-threatening situations alike. It is part of our humanity and is a mechanism that helps us understand when there is something wrong that we should flee. Yet Psalm 46 says that God's presence makes a difference when the world is falling apart all around us. He calms our fears and anxieties in such a way that we can feel safe at the exact moments when physical and emotional safety is often elusive.

God's Presence

As Psalm 46 (NIV) continues, notice the ways in which the writer describes God's presence with a picture: "There is a river whose streams make glad the city of God, the holy place where the Most High dwells. God is within her, she will not fall; God will help her at break of day" (vv. 4–5). These words describe a peaceful scene, as opposed to the chaos of the earlier parts of the passage from which refuge is sought. The picture described is a beautiful city at rest with a serene river quietly flowing through its center. Life is dependent upon water, so most cities around the world were built near a river or other major water source. Consider what G. A. F. Wright says about the possibility that this passage describes Jerusalem:

> Last century, a German professor, in the company of some of his students, dug his way through a blocked up tunnel, out of which water trickled into the Pool of Siloam in the city of Jerusalem. Once they had cleared the long passage of sand and mud, at its very midpoint they found an inscription cut in the wall written in good classical Hebrew. It told how the tunnel, which took an S-bend at one point to suit the layers of the rock, had been started at both ends, and how the workmen had heard each other's picks at that point where the students were now standing. . . . Probably this is the conduit mentioned at 2 Kings 18:17;

20:20; 2 Chron. 32:30, the one beside which the prophet Isaiah took a walk (Isa. 7:3) and ruminated (Isa. 8:5–8). Jerusalem sits on the top of a hard rocky eminence. No rivers can bring it water. But just *outside* the eastern wall, high up, there was a natural spring which they called *Gihon*, which means "gusher." But if the city suffered a siege, the water from the spring remained beyond the reach of the city's inhabitants. So that is why Hezekiah built (or perhaps renovated) this tunnel, in order to feed the waters of Gihon into the Pool of Siloam.

But the spring came gushing up out of— where? There was no river in sight. Gihon was a marvel, a gift from God. . . . This "living" water, as running water is called in Hebrew, can come only from the living God, the giver of life. So even the wrath of the nations cannot move the city that possesses this living water.[6]

Whether this passage describes Jerusalem and the tunnel that brings fresh flowing water from outside no matter how many enemies may besiege it, or whether the passage is merely a figurative reference to describe God's dwelling place, God's presence with His people makes a difference in our world.

Take another look at what the writer says about that city:

1. "God is within her" (v. 5a). God is present in the city. God's presence is what makes

the scene so peaceful. It makes the difference for the inhabitants of the city. God's presence also makes a difference to those who experience traumatic loss. God's presence brings peace and serenity to chaotic times in a supernatural way.

2. ". . . she will not fall" (v. 5a). Because God is present in the city, the inhabitants are secure. There is a tangible difference because God is there. For the inhabitants of ancient Jerusalem, it meant military security. For those who are dealing with the aftermath of traumatic loss, the application of this passage means that the grief does not have to overwhelm you and will not defeat you when God is at your side. Depend upon Him for strength, peace, and security.

3. "God will help her" (v. 5b). This city is said to receive God's assistance through His presence with the inhabitants of the city. Many other times throughout the Bible, readers are told that the Lord is their helper. God indeed helps His people when they are going through difficult, frightening, and challenging times. He provides peace and security because He helps His people.

Let Go!

Trauma, specifically the results of traumatic experiences such as PTSD and particularly moral injury, can make us feel unsettled. We ask questions, we cry out to God, we cling to God for strength, we hope somehow the situation will change, but it does not. We are left looking at the world in the aftermath of grief, loss, and trauma through the eyes of one who feels as though the world no longer makes sense. During such times in life, it is easy to become bitter and jaded. The temptation is to say that God does not care, or that God is not there. But notice what the writer of Psalm 46 (NIV) says, speaking in the first person for God: "Be still, and know that I am God" (v. 10a). Translated by the Christian Standard Bible (CSB), it reads: "Stop fighting, and know that I am God."

I don't know about you, but when my life is in confusion and chaos, the last thing that I want to do is to be still. I want to do something, anything, to change my current situation. I want to make sense of life again and to feel as though I am in control. Yet the instruction here is to be still. Simply know that God exists. There is an old saying that goes, "Let go and let God." But that is not easy. Letting go of our human impulse to *do something* to improve our situation is difficult when things are going normally. After all, we are human beings who want our way, our routines, and our comfort. But in the aftermath of traumatic loss, it can feel impossible to make any difference.

Consider the story of one Vietnam veteran who struggled for decades with alcoholism and relationship problems after his return from war. After years of self-medication, he finally turned to others for help. He went through the Alcoholics Anonymous twelve-step plan and got sober. He consulted Veteran Affairs physicians who prescribed him antidepressants to help him deal with his depression and PTSD. But he said that it wasn't until he finally made peace with God that his life really changed. Today if people ask him about his experience, he points to the sky and says, "I had to take the BIG pill." What he means is that he was able to surrender his hurt and pain to God. He was able to, as the writer of Psalm 46 said, "Be still, and know that I am God" (v. 10 NIV).

God's Power over the Nations

But notice the context of the admonition to "Be still, and know that I am God." These words immediately precede it:

> Come and see what the LORD has done, the desolations he has brought on the earth. He makes wars cease to the ends of the earth. He breaks the bow and shatters the spear; he burns the shields with fire. (vv. 8–9 NIV)

The writer invites us to witness God's activity in the world around us. God is able to put an end to war on earth and can destroy all instruments of war.

We often look at the world around us in a constant state of fear and panic. The world geo-political situation consistently seems unstable, and news reports often leave people anxious about what will happen next. On the local scene, news reports of crime and murder cause fear, distrust, and worry. Nationally, people hear reports of things happening in other regions of the country and develop an "us versus them" mentality. The instruction is meant to calm our inner anxiety and drive us to know that God IS. The fact that God exists and is ultimately in control of the universe should provide a sense of refuge from the rest of the world when chaos surrounds us.

Guided Reflection

The world is frightening. Traumatic grief and loss make everything feel unsteady and uncertain; it leaves us feeling as if there is nothing to which we can cling. It can seem, like the writer of Psalm 46 says, that the mountains are falling into the ocean and all that was familiar and could be grasped is in flux. In such chaos, God Himself is a refuge to those who trust Him. He gives us hope and strength when fear dominates our existence. It is in these moments He offers His presence and tells us to be still and know that He is God despite the chaos in the world that surrounds us. Discuss the following with someone you trust:

1. In the aftermath of your traumatic situation, what makes it the most difficult for you to feel safe?

- How does knowing that God says He is your refuge make a difference?

- What image or scene brings you a sense of peace?

2. What does letting go mean for you *right now*? Revisit this question occasionally when you feel the need for refuge again. Do you notice a pattern of the same answer appearing over time?

Chapter 4

Guidance in the Wilderness

*Even though I walk through the valley
of the shadow of death . . .*
Psalm 23:4 (ESV)

TEMPERATURES SOAR TO 125 DEGREES Fahrenheit. Heat waves create mirages on the horizon. Dirt and rock are the only landscape as far as the eye can see. It looks like one of the opening scenes from the movie *Star Wars,* somewhere on the planet Tatooine. But it is not. It is planet Earth. To be exact, it is western Iraq. In ancient times, this part of Iraq was considered impassible. Early travelers instead followed the Euphrates River north out of Ur and Babylon into what is today northern Syria and southern Turkey. They would then turn south to Lebanon, Israel, and Egypt. Such is the extreme heat and desolation of this area that when Saddam Hussein decided to build a four-lane freeway across this desert to connect Baghdad with Damascus and Ammon, native Iraqis refused. Instead, he contracted with North Korea.

So imagine my amazement one day, as I rode through western Iraq in a US Marine convoy near the Jordanian border, when

GUIDANCE IN THE WILDERNESS

I saw a shepherd in the distance with a herd of sheep. This scene repeated several times over the next few months. Each time I found myself wondering, "What are they eating? There is nothing but dirt and rock out there, and no water." But somehow the sheep survived, and followed their shepherd, who was able to lead them to food and water despite the odds. At one point, I was even told by a group of Iraqi border guards that Anbar Province sheep are the best tasting anywhere in the world. According to them, the harsh conditions create tender and tasty young lambs.

A few months later, I was riding another convoy further east, along the Euphrates River. As we descended from a small hill, I noticed a patch of lush green grass, probably knee-high, next to the river. It was lined with palm trees. In the shade lay a shepherd and a herd of sheep basking in the tranquility of the afternoon. In that moment, familiar words I had heard all my life came flooding into my conscious thoughts, and suddenly made sense as never before:

> The LORD is my shepherd;
> I shall not want.
> He makes me to lie down in green pastures;
> He leads me beside the still waters.
> He restores my soul;
> He leads me in the paths of righteousness
> For His name's sake.
>
> Yea, though I walk through the valley of the
>   shadow of death,
> I will fear no evil;

For You are with me;
Your rod and Your staff, they comfort me.

You prepare a table before me in the presence
    of my enemies;
You anoint my head with oil;
My cup runs over.
Surely goodness and mercy shall follow me
All the days of my life;
And I will dwell in the house of the LORD
Forever. (Psalm 23 NKJV)

Psalm 23 is perhaps the most familiar passage in the Hebrew Bible. It is the most likely to be read during a funeral service or in a hospital room. Perhaps the reason it has become so well-known over the centuries is that its imagery is a source of comfort. The picture of the shepherd herding his sheep is a concrete visual scene, familiar to ancient agrarian cultures. It illustrates how God longs to lead those who will trust Him. It demonstrates the provision of basic physical needs by the shepherd, it describes the shepherd's comforting presence during the most frightening moments, it speaks of restoration and abundance, and ultimately, it points to hope for the future. Psalm 23 is the outline of the ways that God leads and provides for those who trust Him. In the aftermath of horrific trauma, nothing is needed more.

No Fear

Perhaps the best-known phrase of this beloved psalm is: "though I walk through the valley of the shadow of death, I will fear no evil" (v. 4 NKJV). That phrase is significant because the fear of death is something that all human beings share. Treading through dangerous territory and the uncertainty of tragedy, loss, and trauma heighten such feelings.

In 2006 Ramadi was dubbed "the deadliest city in Iraq."[7] Throughout that year, the US military fought for control of the city because of its strategic significance as the capital of the country's largest province.[8] The battle raged for much of the year and into 2007. In early 2008, Marines of the battalion to which I was assigned took over security responsibilities for the Anbar provincial capitol building in downtown Ramadi—the epicenter of much of the previous year's battles. During my first visit to the building, I noticed that a hole, approximately two feet in diameter, had been blown through a concrete wall that was about eight to ten inches thick—likely the result of a rocket-propelled grenade (RPG). Above the hole, someone had inscribed in permanent marker the words of Psalm 23. Interestingly, there was evidence that these words had been written before whatever explosion created the hole. War, terror, and the threat of imminent death heightened the need for those who fought inside this building to be reminded that God was with them as they fought for their lives. For them, this was literally "the valley of the shadow of death" (v. 4 NKJV).

During the summer of 2020, with the COVID-19 pandemic in full motion and the racial tensions following the death of George Floyd fresh in the nation's thoughts, I was called to the emergency room one evening to provide pastoral care for an African American family who had just lost a loved one to the disease. They were stunned and devastated. As I stood with them at the bedside of their deceased loved one, they were silent—stoic. One of them finally broke the silence and said, "2020," and shook his head. I did not immediately understand and asked him to repeat his statement. He spoke more loudly and clearly and repeated, "2020." The message this time was clear. The year 2020 for this family was marked by a global pandemic and racial unrest, all of which was now personified in the death of their loved one. I stood with them in their silence, taking in the gravity of what they were experiencing. After a few moments, I asked if I could read Psalm 23 and then pray with them. They said yes, and I began to read. As I did, they joined in, spontaneously quoting the passage. When I read the phrase above, they began to tear up.

Whether in a war zone or a hospital, the phrase, "though I walk through the valley of the shadow of death, I will fear no evil" (v. 4a NKJV) touches people deeply. Why? Part of the reason can be found in the statement that follows: "For you are with me" (v. 4b NKJV). When trauma, grief, and traumatic loss strike, people are left wondering what happened. They are scared. Fear is normal, but often isolation takes over. Our bodies even have a built-in "fight, flight, freeze" mechanism to help us deal with life-threatening situations. So, back to the imagery of the shepherd and sheep for a moment: Sheep are easily frightened. When a stranger tries to feed them, they often run out of fear. But the familiarity of the voice of their shepherd helps to calm and reassure. The presence of the shepherd makes a difference.

Similarly, life is often threatening to us. Traumatic events can shake us to our core. This passage is comforting because it is a reminder that God is with us even when there is a possibility of imminent death or in the aftermath of traumatic loss. Just like the shepherd calms his sheep, God's presence makes a difference when we have the most to fear!

Peace

But there is more to life than just an absence of fear. Psalm 23 (NKJV) helps us to understand this. It begins by describing a serene scene: "He makes me to lie down in green pastures; he leads me beside the still waters" (v. 2). These two phrases follow another key phrase: "I shall not want" (v. 1b). As I mentioned earlier, sheep startle easily. So, when Psalm 23 describes green pastures and still waters, it describes a place where they can rest and not be frightened of the world around them. The scene is of peace and tranquility where needs for food, water, shelter, and safety are met by a shepherd. In fact, those basic provisions are the primary responsibility of the shepherd. The psalmist is telling us that trusting in God as our Shepherd means trusting that He will provide for our physical needs and help us find safety.

When it comes to trauma recovery, this is significant. Basic care in the aftermath of trauma requires giving attention to our physical needs. Food, water, rest, and safety are necessary parts of life and are vital to restoration. Consider Abraham Maslow's hierarchy of human needs:[9]

Maslow's Hierarchy of Needs

According to Maslow, the human physiological needs for food, water, air, shelter, and sleep must be met even before the needs of safety and security. This means healing from trauma must start with addressing physical needs. No amount of medication or counseling will help someone recover from trauma until their most basic needs have been met. Maybe this is the reason so many cultural customs surrounding death and illness involve food and water. Grief has a way of making us forget that we need to eat and drink. So, when someone dies people take food to the bereaved. In the hospital, friends bring beverages to those experiencing uncertainty and tragedy. It looks like a simple expression of hospitality, but maybe it is more profound. Similarly, the first question that psychiatrists often ask patients experiencing the symptoms of PTSD is: "How are you sleeping?"

One young Iraqi war veteran shared with me his thoughts of suicide. After digging into his story a bit, it was evident he was not getting any sleep and his diet was extremely poor. I helped him connect with the appropriate medical and mental health resources, where he was prescribed medication for his sleep and given dietary recommendations. A couple of weeks later, he appeared to be a completely different person.

Trauma robs us of peace. Yet this psalm is a reminder that God wants to bring peace and serenity back into our lives. He begins by reminding us that we are embodied creatures who have basic physical needs that must be met, just like sheep. Consider how God met basic physical needs in the following story of Israel's prophet Elijah, from the eighth-century BC:

> Elijah was afraid and ran for his life. When he came to Beersheba in Judah, he left his servant there, while he himself went a day's journey into the wilderness. He came to a broom bush, sat down under it and prayed that he might die. "I have had enough, Lord," he said. "Take my life; I am no better than my ancestors." Then he lay down under the bush and fell asleep.

All at once an angel touched him and said, "Get up and eat." He looked around, and there by his head was some bread baked over hot coals, and a jar of water. He ate and drank and then lay down again.

The angel of the LORD came back a second time and touched him and said, "Get up and eat, for the journey is too much for you." So he got up and ate and drank. Strengthened by that food, he traveled forty days and forty nights until he reached Horeb, the mountain of God. (1 Kings 19:3–8 NIV)

Elijah had been on the run for three and half years. He just had a major showdown with 450 prophets of Baal and 400 prophets of Ashtoreth. Then, he outran the king's chariot on a twenty-nine-mile journey—longer than a marathon. If that wasn't enough, his life was threatened, so he escaped into the desert. He experienced stress, exhaustion, isolation, perhaps poor diet, and threat of imminent death. Elijah had reached his breaking point and, "prayed that he might die" (v. 4 NIV). He likely had suicidal thoughts. But notice how God responded to Elijah's prayer for death: There is no reprimand. God simply let him take a long nap. Then He sent an angel with fresh-baked bread and a jug of water. The scene repeated sometime later with more rest, more food, and more water. Do you see the pattern? Before moving on to deal with Elijah's deeper issues, God first provided for his physical needs.

Then, as now, food was central to life. In the ancient world, it was the ultimate sign of hospitality to bring a stranger into one's home and provide them with a meal and a place to stay. In the modern world, gatherings of friends and family are no different. If you want to get to know someone, you invite them to lunch or coffee. When you want to have an enjoyable evening with friends, you have them over for dinner. Throughout history, meeting another human being's need for food is a sign that you care about that person as a human being. Likewise, sleep is often the most significant need of those suffering from PTSD. Hypervigilance—the feeling that you must stay awake to protect yourself and those around you—is a learned behavior in any life-threatening situation. That hypervigilance is a common residual effect for those who have experienced severe trauma. But the need for sleep is paramount. Psychosis and hallucination can occur in those who go too long without it. Finding healing from traumatic experiences requires restorative sleep, as well as food and water, before one can begin to process his or her traumatic experiences.

When Psalm 23 says, "He makes me to lie down in green pastures; He leads me beside the still waters" (v. 2 NKJV), it is a reminder that we are physical beings with physical needs. Just as it is the shepherd's job to lead his sheep and meet their needs, so God longs to meet our physical needs. For Elijah, he did this supernaturally through an angel. In the modern world, God often uses friends, neighbors, family members, churches, doctors, counselors, and many others to meet us where we are and care for our most basic needs. Without proper nutrition and hydration, it is next to impossible to begin healing from trauma. Only when our physical needs have been met can we begin dealing with some of the weightier questions of grief and trauma.

Restoration

As discussed in chapters 1 and 2, the most unsettling part of sudden loss and trauma are the questions and uncertainties they leave behind. Questions such as: "Why did this happen? Why did it happen to me? Did I do something to cause it? Did I fail to do something that could have prevented it? If only I had done [fill-in-the-blank], this would not have happened." Often those questions are the most difficult aspect of dealing with trauma. In recent years, researchers have coined the term *moral injury* to describe some of these feelings and struggles. People who suffer from moral injury long to experience rest, reconciliation, and restoration. Tucked in Psalm 23 is the statement: "He restores my soul" (v. 3 NKJV). God longs to restore our souls and heal the hurt we so often experience in this life.

So how does restoration of the soul take place? It happens in relationship to God. In order to better understand the processes God uses for restoration, let us turn back to Elijah. After the encounter we observed earlier in which God met Elijah's needs, Elijah travels into the desert, where God meets with him.

> There he came to a cave and lodged in it. And behold, the word of the LORD came to him, and he said to him, "What are you doing here,

Elijah?" He said, "I have been very jealous for the Lord, the God of hosts. For the people of Israel have forsaken your covenant, thrown down your altars, and killed your prophets with the sword, and I, even I only, am left, and they seek my life, to take it away." And he said, "Go out and stand on the mount before the Lord." And behold, the Lord passed by, and a great and strong wind tore the mountains and broke in pieces the rocks before the Lord, but the Lord was not in the wind. And after the wind an earthquake, but the Lord was not in the earthquake. And after the earthquake a fire, but the Lord was not in the fire. And after the fire the sound of a low whisper. And when Elijah heard it, he wrapped his face in his cloak and went out and stood at the entrance of the cave. And behold, there came a voice to him and said, "What are you doing here, Elijah?" He said, "I have been very jealous for the Lord, the God of hosts. For the people of Israel have forsaken your covenant, thrown down your altars, and killed your prophets with the sword, and I, even I only, am left, and they seek my life, to take it away." And the Lord said to him, "Go, return on your way to the wilderness of Damascus. And when you arrive, you shall anoint Hazael to be king over Syria. And Jehu the son of

> Nimshi you shall anoint to be king over Israel, and Elisha the son of Shaphat of Abel-meholah you shall anoint to be prophet in your place.... Yet I will leave seven thousand in Israel, all the knees that have not bowed to Baal, and every mouth that has not kissed him." (1 Kings 19:9–16, 18 ESV)

Several things happen in this passage regarding Elijah's restoration. First, God reveals Himself to Elijah in a rather unexpected way. God did not reveal Himself in a grand display of His power; quite the opposite. Notice the refrain: God was not in the wind, He was not in the earthquake, and He was not in the fire.

In Western culture, we have come to expect that bigger is always better. A Big Mac is good, but it's better when the meal is supersized; a concert is great when there are 1,000 people there, but better when there are 60,000. This mentality even invades church life. Churches of 150 people are fine, but why not go to the megachurch with 25,000 people? So, naturally, our modern inclination is that if God is going to restore our souls, there must be some grand experience to punctuate it. That was not the case for Elijah. He heard a gentle whisper and experienced God there instead.

This has been the case in my life as well. God chose a small church of less than fifty people for me to grow and develop and come to know Him as a child and adolescent. He used a small English-speaking church in Europe to call me into ministry. While many of my chaplain colleagues in Iraq led services for large numbers, I led field services on remote border outposts. On one occasion, I led a service for a single Marine on the Jordanian border. God restores our souls through gentle whispers. Sometimes it is something a friend says, at other times it is a song that touches you in a unique way in church. Most of the time, it is a passage of the Bible that, as you read, you know was meant for you in that moment.

Second, God gave Elijah room to ask questions and complain. Elijah's complaints went something like this: "Look God, I have followed You, trusted You. I'm the only one left who's faithful to You, and now they are trying to kill me too." Obviously, things had not turned out the way that Elijah thought they would; he didn't think it was going to be this way. Similarly, trauma can cause us to be disillusioned with life and even with God. It is hard to know what Elijah may have expected, but clearly after being on the run for three years and a major showdown, this was not it. Just like Elijah, we often say, "Life wasn't supposed to turn out this way!" Once I accompanied a casualty officer as he notified a nineteen-year-old young lady that her husband of less than a year had been killed in Iraq. Her first response was that this must be some sort of joke. But when the reality of the situation began to sink in, through her tears, she began to share her dreams of what they thought life was going to look like. As discussed in chapters 1 and 2, part of God's plan for restoration is to allow us space to express our unmet expectations, just as He did for Elijah.

Third, God reminded Elijah that he was not alone. Elijah had complained, "I am the only one left." For more than three years, Elijah had lived mostly isolated and alone. He acutely felt the loneliness of so much time by himself. Trauma and traumatic loss often cause us to feel completely alone, to have a distorted picture of how isolated we are. Yet we are often less isolated than we feel. There are friends, neighbors, family members, and helping agencies that are there—ready, able, and willing to help. In Elijah's case, God corrected his distorted thinking. He informed him that there were still seven thousand people in Israel who had remained faithful to God. When I did clinical rotations in the San Diego VA PTSD clinic, I often saw veterans on their first visit light up when they realized that they were not alone. They met others who experienced the same PTSD symptoms as they did, and that gave them comfort and hope.

Fourth, God commissioned Elijah to go and appoint three leaders. In other words, He gave him a task to complete, work to do. Staying active and maintaining a routine is important in the aftermath of a traumatic loss. One Vietnam veteran I met did not get help for PTSD until after he retired. He had been a workaholic for most of his adult life. He said, "I never had time to think about Vietnam until I retired." While I would not advocate for a level of workaholism that leads to avoidance, having something to do does help you have a sense of purpose. Routines, over time, can ultimately normalize your experiences.

Finally, God gave Elijah a friend and successor. From the very beginning of the Bible God said it is not good to be alone. He created humanity to be in relationship and community with one another and with Himself. Elijah had just spent three and a half years in isolation. God gave Elisha to him as a friend, a successor, and protégé. One young lady who was at high risk of suicide had her life changed when she was introduced to a community of friends in an overseas military chapel. As her sense of aloneness left, so did her thoughts of suicide. Friendships, relationships, and a sense of community are the antidote to aloneness that can change someone's life.

The most pressing need we have in the days, weeks, months, and years after a traumatic experience—after a diagnosis of PTSD or moral injury—is to have our souls restored. Such restoration can only take place in relationship with God (more will be said later about reconciliation with God). But it inevitably involves restoration of relationships with others, a renewed sense of purpose, correction of distorted thinking, and an assurance that we are not alone.

Abundance

Psalm 23 goes on to say, "You prepare a table before me in the presence of my enemies" (v. 5 NKJV). Carey Cash says in his book, *A Table in the Presence,* that the table described in Psalm 23 is symbolic of God's presence and provision:

> The "table" that David spoke about, the "table" that David longed for in the presence of his enemies, was the table of God's presence. It amounted to a feast of spiritual strength and friendship that no degree of danger or no amount

of evil could infringe upon. C. H. Spurgeon said it best a hundred and fifty years ago:

> When a soldier is in the presence of his enemies, if he eats at all, he snatches a hasty meal, and away he hastens to the fight. But observe: "Thou preparest a table," just as a servant does when she unfolds the . . . cloth and displays the ornaments of a feast on an ordinary peaceful occasion. Nothing is hurried: there is no confusion, no disturbance, the enemy is at the front door, and yet God prepares a table.[10]

The imagery of the banquet table in Psalm 23 is indeed a reminder that God's presence and provision is bountiful, even when we are experiencing some of the most horrific and frightening moments of our lives.

Good food is often hard to find when you are in a combat zone. One morning while I was in Iraq, I was waiting for an early helicopter flight to visit Marines in remote areas. As was often the case in buildings used to hold troops waiting for flights around the country, there was a box of Meals Ready to Eat (MREs) in a corner. It was early and I was hungry. What I really wanted was a "real" breakfast. Eggs and bacon or biscuits and gravy were not an option, just whatever MRE could be found in the box. I thought I had struck gold when I found an MRE labeled "Breakfast Omelet." My mouth began to water as I imagined a savory Denver omelet or something similar. I opened the package and took the extra time to use the small heater that would warm the meal by using water and a chemical reaction that produced heat to warm MREs. As I unwrapped the omelet, I imagined the envy of all who sat nearby while I savored such a delicacy. Then came the first bite. It was the most horrible thing that I have ever put in my mouth! The texture was like cottage cheese and the flavor reminded me of rice cakes. In the years since, I have often wondered about that omelet: Was it some disgusting form of powered eggs? Was it real eggs with some weird preservatives? Then I asked myself, *What do you have to do to eggs to make them shelf stable for up to three years?* When the gravity of that question hit, I quickly realized I did not really want an answer!

God does not just offer a disgusting MRE omelet or other mediocre food scraps to sustain us. He gives us more than we could ever imagine we need:

> "Now to him who is able to do above and beyond all that we ask or think according to the power that works in us—to him be glory in the church and in Christ Jesus to all generations, forever and ever. Amen." (Eph. 3:20–21)

Future

Finally, Psalm 23 (NKJV) concludes with two thoughts about the future. The first is: "Surely, goodness and mercy shall follow me all the days of my life" (v. 6a), and the second: "I will dwell in the house of the LORD forever" (v. 6b). These two future-looking statements deal with two realities: The first is the conviction that

God's goodness and mercy will be a part of the person's life for the rest of their time on earth, and the second is that once the author's time on earth is done, he will spend the rest of eternity with God.

One of the most significant ways trauma has an impact upon an individual's life is that it keeps him or her from being able to visualize the future. Duncan Sinclair, in his book *Horrific Traumata*, says, "The person who experiences the full impact of PTSD has been impoverished by the loss of a series of vital spiritual attributes that are essential to living a full life."[11] Included in his list of these ten attributes is "Loss of Future."

Consider the story of a Marine officer who came home from Afghanistan with a traumatic brain injury (TBI) and PTSD. His injury caused him to react angrily toward his family over minor issues. He tried counseling but nothing seemed to be working. Eventually, he began to despair that his life would never change and that nothing could improve. He even began having thoughts of suicide. Then several things happened that changed his course. He found a neurologist who could treat his specific type of TBI. The doctor changed his medications, and he found a different counselor who seemed more able to help. But he said the thing that made the greatest difference was a renewed commitment to his Christian faith. He and his wife began praying together and going to church again with their family. He admits there are still tough days but believes that God is with him. He even gives God credit for helping him to find and receive the medical and mental health treatments that changed his life. Just as David writes in Psalm 23, he believes his life is filled with

God's goodness and mercy. He also believes that he will, "dwell in the house of the LORD forever" (v. 6 NKJV). God has given him a new hope and a future.

Guided Reflection

Psalm 23 is a reminder that recovery from trauma involves meeting very real physical needs for food, water, shelter, and safety. It is also a reminder that recovery from trauma involves the restoration of our very souls that have been damaged and marred. Traumatic events often distort our thinking, leaving us feeling isolated, alone, and purposeless. God often uses common, everyday experiences—rather than dramatic events—to restore us in each of these areas, and in other ways we will see later. God's provision is abundant, even in the middle of our most trying circumstances. Ultimately, He longs for us to experience a life filled with His goodness and mercy so that we can again hope for a bright future with Him. Here is a list of things for you to consider:

1. If you are currently experiencing acute symptoms of PTSD, prioritize your needs for food, water, sleep, exercise, and safety. Take the time to find an appropriate doctor who will help manage any medications that you may need for sleep or depression. And let family and friends help. You and your physicians may need to educate them on what real help means for you at any given time, but do let them.

2. If you are currently wrestling with symptoms of moral injury—feeling as though you could have or should have done something different in your traumatic situation—please invite God to begin restoring your soul. This often starts with thinking differently about the situation. Look back again at the ways that God restored Elijah and ask yourself, "In which of the following ways do I need to allow God to restore me?"

- Stop looking for a dramatic change in life and start looking for the small ways that God is active in your life every day. Write down the small ways you notice when you notice them.
- Continue to bring your real and honest questions to God. He can handle it, and it is okay to do so.
- Ask yourself where your thinking has been distorted, and allow God to restore your thinking. Looking back on things in a new light, you were probably not as able to change things in the situation as you first thought. Take a breath and give yourself a break.
- Realize that you are not as alone as you think you are. Others, while they may not have shared the same experience as you, are likely experiencing similar things. Find ways to connect with them at church,

through support groups, or through veterans and community service agencies.
- Begin building a healthy routine that works for you and allows you to feel productive and active.

Chapter 5

You DO Know!

"Does God even know what is happening to me?"
Anonymous

Sir, I can't take it anymore. Nobody knows what it's really like down here. They think they do, but they only see what is in the news. They don't know what it's like to have the pressure to be perfect all the time; then, get hammered when you slip up just a little bit. I feel like I'm wasting my life, and no one cares! I wish I was in Iraq.

THE ABOVE IS A QUOTE that represents what many have said to me concerning utterances I commonly heard from those who came to talk to me throughout my deployment in Guantanamo Bay, Cuba. For six months I provided pastoral care to the guards and the interrogators inside the Camp Delta detention facility. There was nothing I could do to change anyone's situation. Then, to make a difficult situation even worse, two major international incidents occurred three weeks apart. Just hours before one of these incidents, I stood with a young man who was experiencing an acute reaction to the stress around him. I remember thinking, *I am literally watching this guy develop PTSD before my very eyes!*

So, what do you do? What do you do when you are the military chaplain who is in the center ring of an international drama? Well, I did the only thing that I knew to do: I reminded people that they were not alone, they were not forgotten. God was with them and knew the most intimate details of their lives. Then, I slowly allowed them to express justifiable anger and, finally, to take a look into their own souls. Psalm 139 (NIV) gives a pattern for such an examination:

> You have searched me, LORD,
>   and you know me.
> You know when I sit and when I rise;
>   you perceive my thoughts from afar.
> You discern my going out and my lying down;
>   you are familiar with all my ways.
> Before a word is on my tongue
>   you, LORD, know it completely.
> You hem me in behind and before,
>   and you lay your hand upon me.
> Such knowledge is too wonderful for me,
>   too lofty for me to attain.
>
> Where can I go from your Spirit?
>   Where can I flee from your presence?
> If I go up to the heavens, you are there;
>   if I make my bed in the depths, you are there.

MAKING FRIENDS WITH DARKNESS

If I rise on the wings of the dawn,
    if I settle on the far side of the sea,
even there your hand will guide me,
    your right hand will hold me fast.
If I say, "Surely the darkness will hide me
    and the light become night around me,"
even the darkness will not be dark to you;
    the night will shine like the day,
    for darkness is as light to you.

For you created my inmost being;
    you knit me together in my mother's
    womb.
I praise you because I am fearfully and won-
    derfully made;
    your works are wonderful,
    I know that full well.
My frame was not hidden from you
    when I was made in the secret place.
    when I was woven together in the depths
    of the earth.
Your eyes saw my unformed body;
    all the days ordained for me were written
    in your book
    before one of them came to be.
How precious to me are your thoughts, God!
    How vast is the sum of them!
Were I to count them,

> they would outnumber the grains of
> sand—
> when I awake, I am still with you.
>
> If only you, God, would slay the wicked!
> Away from me, you who are bloodthirsty!
> They speak of you with evil intent;
> your adversaries misuse your name.
> Do I not hate those who hate you, LORD,
> and abhor those who are in rebellion
> against you?
> I have nothing but hatred for them;
> I count them my enemies.
> Search me, God, and know my heart;
> test me and know my anxious thoughts.
> See if there is any offensive way in me,
> and lead me in the way everlasting.

God's Knowledge

When grief, loss, trauma, and life-changing challenges hit, isolation is one of the first things people often feel. For many, such isolation is overwhelming. It feels as though no one else really knows what you are experiencing. Veterans of every war know this to one degree or another. Those who have been sexually assaulted often describe something like an out-of-body experience that they believe no one else understands. Natural disaster victims struggle for words to describe their exposure to the ravages of nature.

Yet, God does know all that is going on in our lives. He knows a level of detail that, if we really think about it, is both comforting and scary at the same time. Notice that Psalm 139 (NIV) says God knows: "When I sit and when I rise," "my thoughts," "my going out and my lying down," "Before a word is on my tongue you . . . know it completely" (vv. 2, 3, 4). God knows the details of our daily routines, including the exact moments we go to bed at night and get up in the morning, He knows our most private and secretive thoughts, the ones that we would never dare tell another soul, and He also knows what we say before we say it. Think about this too: He knows the things we want to say but realize a half second before the words come out of our mouths, that we shouldn't.

While working a summer job during college, I met a lady who said, "I just don't believe there is someone up there keeping track of everything that we do." This lady, for whatever reason, did not want to accept the concept that all her actions and thoughts were known by God. Yet Psalm 139 declares that one of God's attributes is exactly that. He knows on a scale that will blow your mind.

So why does that make a difference? As mentioned earlier, trauma is always isolating. Many people told me during my deployment to Guantanamo Bay that it felt as if no one knew or cared about what they were going through. As a result, they felt alone in what they were experiencing. For example, the daily routine for guards involved a twelve-hour shift filled with consistent barrages of insults from those under their watch. They were constantly on alert for makeshift weapons or other methods of assault. And when guards were either insulted or otherwise physically assaulted, they were not allowed to respond in any way. They could express no sign of anger or emotion. Instead, they were expected to walk away, change into a clean uniform if necessary, and go back to work. Interrogators also had a difficult task. Their job was to solicit information that could prevent another terrorist attack while doing so in a manner that respected the human value and dignity of someone who would kill them and their families, given the opportunity. The geographic and emotional isolation was overwhelming.

The text of Psalm 139 helped some to understand that God knew where they were and what was happening in their lives, despite the geographic and emotional isolation. It brought comfort to know that God understood, even if it felt as though the rest of the world did not. The realization dawned on many as they heard these words that God, indeed, knows what is happening. God knows the intimate details of our lives. What we face each day has not escaped His attention. He knows what each person goes through in the course of life. God knows details when it feels like no one else does, or cares!

Consider the story of one young man who, in the middle of all of what was described above, received divorce papers from his wife. He wondered aloud how he was going to cope and whether he could go on with life. How could he continue in such a high-stakes deployment when everything at home was falling apart? He struggled to find meaning and purpose. Upon hearing the words of Psalm 139, he recognized that while nothing in his life had changed, at least God knew where he was and what was happening. That gave him enough courage to forge ahead through the difficult path before him.

And that's the point. The situations in our lives may not change, and we may still feel alone and isolated because of traumatic experiences. But the knowledge that the same God who created the universe knows the intimate details of our lives makes a difference. It helps us face life when we might otherwise give up.

God's Presence

But there is more to this psalm than just God's knowledge. God not only knows what we experience, He is there with us as we experience it. In fact, David, the writer of Psalm 139 (NIV), asks: "Where can I go from your Spirit? Where can I flee from your presence?" (v. 7). The response to his question is this:

> If I go up to the heavens, you are there;
>   if I make my bed in the depths, you are there.
> If I rise on the wings of the dawn,
>   if I settle on the far side of the sea,
> even there your hand will guide me,
>   your right hand will hold me fast.
>   (vv. 8–10)

Essentially, he is saying, "God, I haven't yet found the place where I can get away from your presence."

In the movie *The Martian*, the main character Mark Watney (played by Matt Damon) reflects on his life alone on Mars.

He looks around the landscape and contemplates. He says, "Everywhere I go, I'm the first. It's a strange feeling. Step outside the rover? First guy to be there. Climb that hill? First guy to do that. Four and a half billion years—nobody here. And now—me. I'm the first person to be alone on an entire planet."[12] Whether it is the surface of Mars, Guantanamo Bay, the deserts of Iraq, the mountains of Afghanistan, the jungles of Vietnam, the loneliness of a prison cell, the isolation of a hospital room, or at the scene of a disaster, accident, or assault, God is there. God has already been in all the places we could ever go on this planet or any other.

As modern readers, we see the phrase "if I make my bed in the depths" (v. 8) much like the old saying, "You have made your bed, now lie in it." While the context does allow for that interpretation, the original language goes further. Some translations of the Bible include the original Hebrew word *Sheol*, which refers to the place of the dead. The best modern understanding we have of the concept of Sheol is that it was the place outside a city where trash was dumped and burned, burning continuously. It was also the place where bodies were burned that were not claimed and buried by family. It gives new meaning to the phrase "burn pits." It was considered the place of the dead. Some Bible translations translate "Sheol," as "hell." So, what the writer is saying, in essence, is something like this: "God, even if I have made my bed in the pits of hell, in the place of the dead, You are still there with me."

Those who have experienced the nightmares and horrors of war, natural disaster, sexual assault, or other acts of violence know what the author means. They have experienced depravity, inhumanity, and loss. Such devastation is oppressive. It can feel as though life can never change, that it will always be as dark as what you are experiencing right now. Trauma has a way of making people feel isolated physically and emotionally. But the point of this passage is that there is no place you can ever go that God is not already there—no matter how deep and dark the pit in which you find yourself! God is with you even in the darkest pit of your life! Perhaps this is why the author continues with thoughts about God's presence and darkness:

> If I say, "Surely the darkness will hide me
>   and the light become night around me,"
> even the darkness will not be dark to you;
>   the night will shine like the day,
>   for darkness is as light to you.
> (vv. 11–12 NIV)

In these two sections of the passage, the author is asking, "Is there anywhere I can go that God is not?" and "Is there anywhere that I can actually hide from God?" Darkness cannot hide one from God, nor can circumstances or isolation ever take one so far away from God that He is not already there.

Dark moments in life often cause people to turn to things that they think will mask or hide the pain and/or guilt that they may be feeling because of traumatic events. Many of the Vietnam vets I worked with spent decades after the war trying to numb their pain with alcohol and substance abuse, only to find that the pain was still there. Veterans from the Iraq and Afghan wars were often known to become adrenaline junkies, taking increasingly dangerous risks in order to "feel alive," but in doing so, bury their emotions related to their traumatic memories. Similarly, survivors of sexual assault sometimes numb their pain through substance abuse and other reckless behaviors to distance themselves from their feelings. It is as if, after experiencing pain and darkness, they want to further hide their emotions in the darkness around them. Those who suffer from such traumatic memories often feel isolated from the world around them and even from a fully integrated view of themselves. Many suffer from moral injury, blaming themselves for situations that they may or may not have been able to control.

Darkness comes in all shapes and forms. On the surface it would seem that darkness begets darkness. Some people who have experienced a traumatic event say to themselves and those around them, "But you weren't there. You don't understand." Such logic seems to say, "Something dark has happened to me, and no one will ever understand or accept me afterward, so just let me hide in the darkness." This is exactly what the writer of Psalm 139 was feeling. He said, "Surely the darkness will hide me," only to realize that God can see through the darkness around us as if it were daylight.

Neither the darkness of the night of trauma, nor the distance from anything familiar—or anything else—means that God is not there. God is always present with us. He is present in the deepest and darkest pit of our lives. There is no place in the universe where we could go to escape Him. Darkness does not hide us from Him, nor do our dark circumstances mean that He is not with us. He sees, knows, and walks with us through the most difficult moments of our lives. God's presence is always with us. Such perspective gives us the strength we need to deal with life's most difficult moments.

God's Creation

While God knows all the intimate details of each of our lives and is always present with us, there is more. Our very lives are a gift from God. Notice what the author of Psalm 139 says:

> For you created my inmost being;
> > you knit me together in my mother's womb.
>
> I praise you because I am fearfully and wonderfully made;
> > your works are wonderful,
> > I know that full well.
>
> My frame was not hidden from you
> > when I was made in the secret place.
> > when I was woven together in the depths of the earth.
>
> Your eyes saw my unformed body;
> > all the days ordained for me were written
> > in your book
> > before one of them came to be.
>
> (vv. 13–16 NIV)

Notice the perspective of this passage: God knew the details of our lives before we were conceived. He knows all that we will experience in life—the good, the bad, and the ugly. He was intimately acquainted with and even supervised our physical development. He knows the exact moment of our deaths. He knows everything in between. We are His special creation.

Traumatic times feel as if they will last forever, and the aftermath of trauma leaves us feeling as though our lives will never be the same. During many deployments in very different locations around the world, I would often ask people, "How's it going today?" The response was often the same: "It's Groundhog Day."[13] The feeling that every day is the same and that nothing ever changes is a common feeling for those deployed in the military in general. But when tragedy strikes, the emotional pain leaves people feeling as though the pain will never end!

While traumatic events are overwhelming at the time they occur and can often consume our lives even in the aftermath, it helps to define them, to limit their scope and impact on our lives by the way we think and talk about them. Traumatic events are but a small snapshot of our lives in comparison to the totality of a lifetime. There is healing in reviewing them and the impact they made on our lives, then reminding ourselves that those events are but one small part of our lives and need not dictate who we are as human beings. God has already done that. He has said in this passage that we are "fearfully and wonderfully made" (v. 14 NIV). In other words, traumatic events do not define who we are—God gets to do that. He reminds us that we are His creatures and that we have value for that reason; He loves us and created us.

One officer frequently encouraged those under his charge by saying,

> Don't let this place kick your butt. The time that you are here, compared with the totality of the length of your life is really small. So try to put this place in perspective and realize that someday you will tell your grandchildren stories about it.

The strategy seemed to work for many and is a tiny illustration of what the psalmist is saying. God has given us life. He knows us and is present with us. He tells us that we are His unique creations. He has fixed limits on our very lives and, by extension, has also limited the amount of time that our suffering takes place. It is important, therefore, that we do not allow our suffering to dominate our lives any more than it needs to. (More on this in chapter 6.)

We are finite creatures with a beginning and an end in this world. That also means that we have physical bodies with limitations. We are emotional creatures that can be stretched to the point of breaking through the stress of life's traumatic events. It is significant that, after reminding His reader about God's infinite knowledge and His presence everywhere, David reminds us we are God's created beings. He knows and defines the limits of our "creatureliness," and He watches over us with the eye of the Master Craftsman, looking after all of the intimate details of who we are. That perspective helps us define the events of our lives and understand them in the proper context.

Anger

So, what does all this mean for those who have experienced life's deepest pits? It means God has not forgotten you. It means that He knows and is intimately familiar with human suffering—yours included. He knows the suffering you endured, suffering you were not able to prevent, and suffering you may have caused. Several Iraq war veterans shared with me the details of situations in which they caused the death of innocent civilians. In each case, they were told by leaders that they did what was necessary to protect those around them. But living with the knowledge that you caused the deaths of innocents can be brutal. It causes anger. That anger may be expressed in rage at oneself, or the state of the world, that the situation could not be changed.

One Iraq war veteran who was struggling with reintegrating into stateside life said, "Sometimes I just want to scream at people and say, 'Have you ever killed someone? Well, I have, so I don't care about what you think is important today, and your little rules about things that don't matter. . . .'" His anger reflects what many feel upon returning home, knowing that their service caused pain and suffering for others.

There are many types of anger. Righteous indignation is anger toward evil and injustice that are all too often found in our world. Those who have experienced the pain associated with injustices, often because of traumatic situations, know this indignation well. David, in Psalm 139 (NIV), describes it this way:

> If only you would slay the wicked!
> Away from me, you who are bloodthirsty!

> They speak of you with evil intent;
>   your adversaries misuse your name.
> Do I not hate those who hate you, Lord,
>   and abhor those who are in rebellion
>   against you?
> I have nothing but hatred for them;
>   I count them my enemies. (vv. 19–22)

David's desire is for God's judgment and wrath to fall upon the wicked. If we are honest with ourselves, every human has experienced this desire in one form or another. We see injustice and wickedness, and are confused about why God continues to allow suffering. We wonder why He allows the wicked to seemingly go unpunished. Look again at how these wicked people are described. He says that they are "bloodthirsty," they speak of God with "evil intent," and they "misuse [God's] name" (vv. 19–20). His response to these people was one of hatred: "I count them my enemies" (v. 22).

Veterans from nearly every war can identify with such visceral emotions. There is often hatred toward an enemy who has taken the lives of friends. Maybe it is anger and resentment toward political leaders that lead a nation into war, or anger at those who make costly mistakes while leading in wartime. As I write these words, it is December 7. Throughout the day, I have seen scores of news articles and social media postings that remind us of the Japanese attacks on Pearl Harbor, the day President Franklin Roosevelt famously said would "live in infamy."

Similarly, veterans of both the Vietnam and Afghanistan wars, in particular, often express anger at how the United States pulled out of those respective countries, leaving innocents behind to suffer, and leaving those who served to wonder what their sacrifices had accomplished. Certainly, there was anger among those with whom I served in Guantanamo Bay. Korean War veterans often describe their anger about being the "forgotten war." I experienced a similar kind of anger when the Anbar Province capitol building in Ramadi, Iraq, fell under ISIS control in 2015. As mentioned in chapter 4, I had visited this building multiple times in earlier years, even standing on the roof with no flak jacket or helmet. Doing that would have been suicidal prior to the Anbar Awakening.[14] Seeing a previously secure capitol building fall under ISIS control was just too much.

Some suggest these words of anger should not be in Psalm 139, that they somehow interrupt the flow of such a beautiful and poetic description of God's intimate knowledge of humanity. I disagree. God's knowledge of humanity cannot be complete without an acknowledgment of the anger we so often experience at the hurt and pain around us. If God knows the most intimate details of our lives, if His presence goes with us into the darkest places on earth, if He knows our lives from before the moment we were conceived, the exact moment of our deaths, and everything in between, then He is surely acquainted with our anger at the difficulties faced in this world.

What the psalmist is expressing is a righteous anger: "Do I not hate those who hate you, Lord" (v. 21 NIV). Longing for justice is a natural human desire. We desire for everything in the world to be set right again—to be rid of those who hate and rebel against God, and who cause nothing but pain and destruction. Yet history is replete with such hatred.

Introspection

Perhaps this is why Psalm 139 (NIV) ends the way it does. Imagine a pause between the statement "I count them my enemies" (v. 22) and what follows: "Search me, God, and know my heart; test me and know my anxious thoughts. See if there is any offensive way in me, and lead me in the way everlasting" (vv. 23–24). It is as if the author takes a breath from his anger, recognizes that he cannot control others, and then asks God to examine him. Anger and resentment are normal reactions to injustice. Yet try as we might, we cannot change the past, nor can we change the attitudes and behaviors of others. The only thing each of us can control is ourselves. Even then, we have difficulty. We need a guide with greater insight, one who can really see into the deep recesses of our hearts, to help us root out anger, bitterness, and resentment we often face at the injustices of life.

Those who experience trauma and moral injury find themselves wrestling not only with the anger associated with loss, but often with the feelings that they, too, bear blame for failing to prohibit the event. There is anger, hatred, resentment, guilt, and a score of other emotions that fill this space. Consider the story of one young man who was involved in the death of an innocent civilian in a combat zone. His leaders assured him that he had done the right thing by protecting those around him. He followed the rules of engagement, and he and his buddies lived and made it home. But someone who was innocent died as a result of his actions, and that was more than he could live with. His guilt and shame were overwhelming. He was angry at himself, angry at the situation, even angry with those who continued to tell him that he had done the right thing.

The only thing that can help that type of shame and guilt is the kind of open examination the writer of Psalm 139 begs of God. It is as if he comes to the end of his angry tirade and then pauses to say, "But God, I want you to take a deep look into my heart." That's huge. It is no small thing to say to the creator God—who sees all and knows all—"Examine me."

Why would he say this? One of the things I have learned through the course of my life is how little control I actually have. Control is an illusion at best. We cannot control the actions or responses of other people. We cannot control the events in our lives or in the lives of those around us. At the end of the day, the only thing we can (almost) control is ourselves. It seems the author of Psalm 139 shares this realization. So, he says to God, "Examine me, point out my anxious thoughts. Lead me in your ways" (see vv. 23–24). Such is the main theme of Psalm 139. God is the only one who sees and knows everything there is to know about us. He is the only one qualified to point out our anxieties, hurts, and frustrations. He is also the only one who can do anything about it. That's why the concluding prayer is simply, "God, show me where I need to change and teach me your ways."

Guided Reflection

---

1. Make a list of the things in your life that you now recognize that God knows about you. Include those things that others already know about you and then add the things that no other human being knows. Pray with God as you review the list and thank Him that He already knows these things about you. You may feel it necessary to burn the list afterward to protect your privacy. That's okay. God still knows. Hopefully that knowledge will make it easier for you to move on.

2. List some (or all) of the ways that you have tried to hide your guilt and feelings from others and God. Have you succeeded in actually hiding anything from God?

3. Consider your anger and resentment related to your traumatic experiences with these questions:

- What are you most angry about?
- What are you most resentful of?
- Is your anger and resentment justified?
- Is it helping anyone? Who is it hurting?

Now, make a list of the ways that your anger and resentment have been productive. Have they produced any change?

4. Are you willing to say to God, "Please look deep into my life and point out to me the ways in which I need to change"? If you're not able to ask Him that yet, what is keeping you from doing so?

Chapter 6

Choices

> *"Everything can be taken from a man but one thing: the last of the human freedoms— to choose one's attitude in any given set of circumstances, to choose one's own way."*[15]
> Viktor Frankl, *Man's Search for Meaning*

AUSTRIA, 1942: A YOUNG JEWISH psychiatrist by the name of Viktor Frankl was arrested by the Nazis along with his family. Throughout World War II, Frankl spent three years in four different German concentration camps. Ultimately, his parents, his wife, and his brother all died in captivity. Before the war, Frankl was a student under both Sigmund Freud and Alfred Adler. Prior to his arrest, Frankl had the opportunity to escape to New York, but said that he could not abandon his parents to their fate. Frankl knew firsthand what it was like to lose everything— his family, his freedom, his possessions, and his position. As a trained psychiatrist who endured life in the concentration camps, Frankl not only experienced these losses himself, but he also observed others and their reactions as they endured one of the most inhuman environments the world has ever known. What he concluded was profound. He said there was one freedom that can never be taken from a person: the ability to choose how to respond to one's circumstances. His idea was that if you were to take everything from a person, even strip him naked, that person still has the freedom to choose how to respond to such losses. No one can ever touch the freedom to choose how you respond.

Frankl said that he was able to endure the harsh conditions of his imprisonment only by imagining himself someday lecturing in front of large crowds about what he had learned and endured as a prisoner of war (POW). That is exactly what he did. When the war was over and he was released, he wrote about his experiences. His book, *Man's Search for Meaning*, is a worldwide bestseller. Frankl spent the rest of his life teaching and lecturing on what he learned about human behavior during his concentration camp experience.

Ancient Israel's King David was no stranger to fear and loss. Early in his life, he faced threats to his life from his father-in-law, and predecessor, King Saul. As a result, he lived in exile for years, on the run for his life, surrounded by a band of loyal warriors. After a few years, Saul died, and David became king. But midway through David's forty-year reign, he was on the run again. This time, his own son Absalom conspired against him and led an armed rebellion and coup attempt. All-out war ensued and Absalom was killed by the commander of David's army. David won the war and was reinstated as king, but lost a son.

There were other times too. God helped David miraculously escape on many occasions. Just prior to facing Goliath, he boasted to Saul that he had killed a lion and a bear with his bare hands. But David was human. He got tired of being on the run. He became exhausted mentally, physically, and emotionally. Like many of us, he wondered where his life was going and if God would ever answer any of his prayers. There was pain in the depths of his soul. He longed for God to restore him, protect him, and defend his reputation. Yet in the middle of all of this, he made a choice to continue trusting God despite all indications to the contrary. David wrote the following poem about his struggle in Psalm 13:

> O Lord, how long will you forget me?
>> Forever?
>> How long will you look the other way?
> How long must I struggle with anguish in my
>> soul,
>> with sorrow in my heart every day?
>> How long will my enemy have the upper
>> hand?
>
> Turn and answer me, O Lord my God!
>> Restore the sparkle to my eyes, or I will
>> die.
> Don't let my enemies gloat, saying, "We have
>> defeated him!"
>> Don't let them rejoice at my downfall.
>
> But I trust in your unfailing love.
>> I will rejoice because you have rescued me.
> I will sing to the Lord
>> because he is good to me. (NLT)

Forgotten

This psalm returns to the themes of chapters 1 and 2, specifically the feelings of being forgotten by God. Notice the questions that David has for God: "How long will you forget?" "How long must I struggle?" "How long will others have the upper hand?" When trauma, grief, and sudden loss come, those questions become the primary concerns in our lives. Our desperation boils down to something like, "God, how long is this horror going to last? You have completely forgotten me!" Even though passages like the one that we examined in the last chapter remind us that God has not forgotten us, it still can feel as though He has. Our questions remain because the pain remains. We want resolution and we feel as though we have been forgotten. We want God to act and, like David, we ask, "Is this going to go on forever?"

You have probably experienced such times in your life, the times when you think: *Is this ever going to end?* Just this morning I read an article about the war in Ukraine. A team of journalists had shadowed a group of doctors in a Ukrainian military hospital on the front lines. Their description of daily life in the hospital was like the movie *Groundhog Day*, meaning every day was the same. The doctors they spoke with seemed to have lost track of time. They knew nothing but the daily grind of triage, stabilization, and surgery. They had no idea how long this would last. They were in constant danger and yet took great risks to save the lives of others. When asked about their decision to stay and provide medical care, they said that they could do nothing else, it was their duty. But in such an environment, it would be easy to feel forgotten. David wrote about such feelings and pleaded with God; he longed for God to act and resolve his situation.

Restoration

We want resolution. But what we long for is restoration. We want things to go back to normal. We want the situation that interrupted our lives to go away, and things to be restored to the way they were prior to the trauma. We want life to carry on with some sense of normalcy. The phrase that stands out more than anything to me in this passage is this: "Restore the sparkle to my eyes, or I will die" (v. 3 NLT). We know the "sparkle" in someone's eye when we see it. It represents a zest for life—a passion, motivation, and energy to accomplish things and to enjoy life. Think about the "sparkle" in instances like these: a twelve-year-old boy getting ready to play a practical joke on his sister; a groom on his wedding day when he catches the first glimpse of his bride walking down the aisle; a young mother holding her newborn baby for the very first time. The "sparkle in the eye" is the image of a healthy person whose vitality and ability to thrive in the world is evident when you look into their eye. David pleads with God for a restoration of that health and vitality when he says, "Restore the sparkle to my eyes, or I will die" (v. 3 NLT). For David this is not hyperbole. He is begging God for a change, and sees little way to go on unless God acts!

During the early days of the COVID-19 pandemic, people struggled to make sense of what was happening to the world and the lives they had known prior. Lockdowns created loneliness and depression. In online forums people talked about the difficulties they had with isolation, and the challenges of not being able to do simple things like go to work every day and the inability to be around family. Like David, we wanted our lives to get back to normal; to a full, thriving life in the midst of dramatic change. David pleaded with God: "If you don't restore me, I'm gonna die!" (v. 3b, paraphrased). Perhaps that's where you are right now. You feel as though you are going to die if something doesn't change soon. You see no future in your current circumstances and feel there is no way life can go on unless something changes. Yet, time stretches on, and your "new normal" is still there.

Saving Face

After times like these go on for a while, it is natural to look around and wonder why your life is different from others. Some people go one step further and begin to suspect what others around them may be saying behind their backs. They question whether other people are blaming them for their circumstances. One example in the Bible comes from the life of Job. He lost everything: wealth, possessions, ten children, and his health. His friends came to sit with him and comfort him. But after seven days they could no longer contain themselves, and accusations began. They told him it was his fault. They said that bad things don't happen to good people, so he should confess his sin to God and be done with his suffering. I've heard many people say similar things. David says it this way: "Don't let my enemies gloat!" (v. 4 NLT).

When sudden tragedy strikes there are sometimes questions about what others are thinking. Often the question is turned inwardly: "What did I do wrong?" I knew a man who was involved in a large truck accident. When he woke up in the hospital, he said, "I must have done something wrong for God to let this happen." Likewise, I visited a woman in a hospital once immediately after she had received news that she had cancer. Her question was the same: "What did I do wrong, that God gave me cancer?" Sudden trauma and loss can leave us with the feeling that everyone around us is looking at us, wondering the same question—particularly our critics. David felt this too and cried out to God, "Let this end so that my enemies won't get the upper hand" (v. 4, paraphrased).

Choices

But the crux of this passage may be in what is not there. Take a look at the very next thing David says. In one sentence we read, "Don't let them rejoice at my downfall" (v. 4 NLT). In the very next breath he says, "But I trust in your unfailing love" (v. 5 NLT). Nothing was different. There is no indication that David's circumstances had changed. There is no evidence of God's rescue, no hint that anything in David's life was different. The only thing we see is a deliberate choice: "But I trust. . . ." David chose to trust God when life did not make sense. Just as Viktor Frankl said that the last of the human freedoms is the ability to choose how to respond to our circumstances, David made the choice to choose to trust God despite his difficulties.

How do you make that mental shift? The shift from thinking God has forgotten you, longing for God's restoration, struggling to save face—then suddenly shift to trusting God? That sounds easier that it is. Stories of people trusting God in impossible circumstances have always fascinated me. Years ago, I saw a video about POWs in Vietnam, whose Christian faith sustained them through the years of torture and isolation. In each of their stories, there was a choice—a moment they could articulate—when they chose to continue to trust God despite their circumstances. Through the centuries, there have also been many other such stories. Church history is filled with accounts of those who chose to trust God even when doing so meant certain death.

In Psalm 13, David makes a conscious choice to trust God. There are three things that seem to influence his decision to trust God: God's unfailing love; the memory of how God had rescued him in the past; and the conviction that, despite his situation, God had been good to him. Each of those things are worth some exploration below.

Unfailing Love

Evidence of God's love abounds through the Scriptures and through ancient Israel's story. It was the first thing David thought about when deciding to trust God. God's love was familiar to him. In fact, a quick search of the Bible reveals that the phrase *unfailing love* appears 121 times. Look at just a few of these occurrences from the writings of Moses:

- "Praise the LORD, the God of my master, Abraham," he said. "The LORD has shown ***unfailing love*** and faithfulness to my master, for he has led me straight to my master's relatives." (Gen. 24:27 NLT, emphasis added)
- "With your ***unfailing love*** you lead the people you have redeemed. In your might, you guide them to your sacred home." (Exod. 15:13 NLT, emphasis added)
- "But I lavish ***unfailing love*** for a thousand generations on those who love me and obey my commands." (Exod. 20:6 NLT, emphasis added)
- The LORD passed in front of Moses, calling out, "Yahweh! The LORD! The God of compassion and mercy! I am slow to anger and filled with ***unfailing love*** and faithfulness." (Exod. 34:6 NLT, emphasis added)
- "I lavish ***unfailing love*** to a thousand generations. I forgive iniquity, rebellion, and sin. But I do not excuse the guilty. I lay the sins of the parents upon their children and grandchildren; the entire family is affected—even children in the third and fourth generations." (Exod. 34:7 NLT, emphasis added)

- "The LORD is slow to anger and filled with ***unfailing love***, forgiving every kind of sin and rebellion. But he does not excuse the guilty. He lays the sins of the parents upon their children; the entire family is affected—even children in the third and fourth generations." (Num. 14:18 NLT, emphasis added)
- "In keeping with your magnificent, ***unfailing love***, please pardon the sins of this people, just as you have forgiven them ever since they left Egypt." (Num. 14:19 NLT, emphasis added)
- "But I lavish ***unfailing love*** for a thousand generations on those who love me and obey my commands." (Deut. 5:10 NLT, emphasis added)
- "Understand, therefore, that the LORD your God is indeed God. He is the faithful God who keeps his covenant for a thousand generations and lavishes his ***unfailing love*** on those who love him and obey his commands." (Deut. 7:9 NLT, emphasis added)
- "If you listen to these regulations and faithfully obey them, the LORD your God will keep his covenant of ***unfailing love*** with you, as he promised with an oath to your ancestors." (Deut. 7:12 NLT, emphasis added)

The bottom line is this: It was well-known and established that God is a God of unfailing love. God's unfailing love was evident in Abraham's life when he sent his servant to find a wife for his son.[16] It was evident when Moses led Israel out of captivity in Egypt, through the Red Sea,[17] and across forty years of wandering in the desert.[18] It was present in the commands handed down on Mount Sinai, and in the covenant promises God made with the people of Israel.[19] David was aware of all of this. He probably also thought about his own experiences with God's unfailing love: victory over Goliath, the anointing as king by the prophet Samuel, and many others when he had personally seen God's unfailing love in his own life. So, he chose to trust in God even though he could not see the evidence of God in the moment.

That statement encapsulates much of life. It is often difficult to see God's activity in the moment. For some of us that causes doubt and disbelief. For others, it is a crisis. Nevertheless, there is always a decision to be made: choose to trust God even when it does not make sense, or turn away. Over the years I have seen people on both sides of this decision. Tragedy strikes, and the first reaction is often one of despair.

For example, all my life I had heard the saying, "There are no atheists in foxholes." I had taken this statement as absolute truth. Yet when I deployed to Iraq, I saw something different. What I found instead was that war magnifies one's beliefs about God. Those who believed in God had their faith strengthened and deepened as they trusted Him for their very survival. On the other hand, questions and doubts about God before combat often grew into full-blown hostility toward God, fanning the flames of agnosticism and atheism. What separated these individuals was their belief about God's love. Those who knew of God's unfailing love often continued to trust Him. Others simply scoffed at the idea of God's love. They insisted that IEDs killing friends, and terrorists acting in the name of religion, was ample evidence that God, if He did exist, was cruel, not loving. There were exceptions to these patterns, for sure, but the question of God's unfailing love was pivotal in how people responded to combat.

A few years ago, I visited a family in the hospital room of a loved one who had just passed away. It had been a long battle with a serious disease, but the family member's death had still come sooner than anyone expected. Before the visit, I had been given the details and was prepared for a family in significant distress. What I found instead, when I walked into the room, was a family who was thankful for their loved one, thankful for the years with him, and thankful for the assurance that they would see him again someday because of God's unfailing love. In short, they were sad because of his death but also exhibited genuine faith in God's love that provided them peace.

Previous Rescue

It is not just God's unfailing love, though, that causes David to choose to trust Him. He says, "You have rescued me" (Ps. 13:5 NLT). This statement could be taken multiple ways. Perhaps David meant, "I'm confident, God, that You will ultimately rescue me." However, the past tense of the statement more likely refers to times in the past when God had already rescued David, and David was reflecting on those times. It is hard to tell what occasions David may have been thinking about. But here are a few possibilities:

As a young man, David volunteered to fight Goliath. Saul argues that David is too young and inexperienced to fight him:

> "Don't worry about this Philistine," David told Saul. "I'll go fight him!"
>
> "Don't be ridiculous!" Saul replied. "There's no way you can fight this Philistine and possibly win! You're only a boy, and he's been a man of war since his youth."
>
> But David persisted. "I have been taking care of my father's sheep and goats," he said. "When a lion or a bear comes to steal a lamb from the flock, I go after it with a club and rescue the lamb from its mouth. If the animal turns on me, I catch it by the jaw and club it to death. I have done this to both lions and bears, and I'll do it to this pagan Philistine, too, for he has defied the armies of the living God! The LORD who **rescued me** from the claws of the lion and the bear will **rescue me** from this Philistine!" (1 Sam. 17:32–37a NLT, emphasis added)

Later in the same passage, the Bible reveals that God did, indeed, rescue David:

> David replied to the Philistine, "You come to me with sword, spear, and javelin, but I come to you in the name of the LORD of Heaven's Armies—the God of the armies of Israel, whom you have defied. Today the LORD will conquer you. . . . And everyone assembled here will know that the **LORD rescues** his people, but not with sword and spear. This is the LORD's battle, and he will give you to us!"
>
> As Goliath moved closer to attack, David quickly ran out to meet him. Reaching into his shepherd's bag and taking out a stone, he hurled it with his sling and hit the Philistine in the forehead. The stone sank in, and Goliath stumbled and fell face down on the ground.
>
> So David triumphed over the Philistine with only a sling and a stone, for he had no sword. (vv. 45–50 NLT, emphasis added)

Then in the next chapters, Saul's jealousy of David boils over:

> The very next day a tormenting spirit from God overwhelmed Saul, and he began to rave in his house like a madman. David was playing the harp, as he did each day. But Saul had a spear in his hand, and he suddenly hurled it at David, intending to pin him to the wall. But David escaped him twice. (18:10–11 NLT)

Whether it was any of these incidents or others that David was thinking about when he wrote the words of Psalm 13, we will never know. The point is that David had seen God rescue him and others in the past, and he was confident as he thought about his current situation. He deliberately chose to believe that God could still rescue him. Perhaps you have had some of those experiences. I have. On at least two occasions, God has rescued me from near death.

The first was the event I described in chapter 3, when a small branch in exactly the right place, at exactly the right time, saved me from falling into an abandoned uranium mine. The second was a car accident that should have taken my life and did not. It was late one night in New Mexico. I had left San Diego at around 5:00 a.m. and was determined to get to our new house in Oklahoma in one day. It was Valentine's Day, and I wanted to see my wife. It had been raining for hours. The area of Interstate 40 where I was driving had deep ruts worn in both lanes from the volume of traffic. With the rain, the ruts had filled with water. As I was passing a semitruck, near the midsection of its trailer, my car hydroplaned. I tried correcting, but nothing happened. More correction—still nothing.

Finally, as I was about to hit the median, my front tires caught traction. However, the tires were turned from my attempts to correct, and the front of my car took a hard right and headed underneath the semitruck's trailer. I remember thinking, *Okay, this is how I'm going to die!* Followed quickly by the prayer, "Lord, please make it quick and painless." At that moment, the rear tire of the trailer hit the right front of my car. It knocked me out from under the trailer. I spun 360 degrees and ended up in the right lane pointed at a forty-five-degree angle toward the other ditch. An hour later, as I stood with a New Mexico state trooper (who was writing me a ticket), I shivered at the thought: *I guess God still has a plan and purpose for my life!* I believe He rescued me from almost certain death. The trooper later admitted to me that he took his time getting to the accident scene because he was not anxious to see the carnage that he expected from such an accident. In fact, he was shocked that I was alive and standing before him, given what he had been told of the accident on his police radio.

Perhaps you have similar stories of God's rescue in your life. In the aftermath of trauma and traumatic loss, it can sometimes be hard to think about anything other than your present circumstances. David chose to reflect on the times God had previously rescued him, and then chose to believe that God would and could still rescue him, even when nothing seemed to be changing.

God's Goodness

The choice to trust God involved a reflection on God's unfailing love, remembering occasions of God's rescue, and the nature of God's goodness. David wraps up Psalm 13 by saying, "I will sing to the LORD because he is good to me" (v. 6 NLT). It seems David was saying that part of his choice to trust God was a belief that—despite everything—God is still good.

Nineteenth-century pastor and evangelist Charles Spurgeon said it this way: "The worldling blesses God while he gives him plenty, but the Christian blesses him when he smites him: he believes him to be too wise to err and too good to be unkind; he trusts him where he cannot trace him, looks up to him in the darkest hour, and believes that all is well."[20]

Some translations of this part of Psalm 13 render it: "You have dealt bountifully with me."[21] Think about that for a minute. Think about the incredible bounty of God's creation. Think about the ways in which God has dealt bountifully with His people throughout history. How does His bounty reflect the goodness of His nature?

In the very first chapters of the Bible is the story of the account of creation. After each successive day of creation, we read the refrain: "it was good." Then when everything is complete, the refrain changes slightly: "it was very good." Adam and Eve are enjoying a completely carefree life, living in the bounty of all that God has created, and are in absolute peace.

Later, when the Israelites are exiting Egypt and wandering in the wilderness, God promises that He will lead them into "a land flowing with milk and honey" (Exod. 3:8; Num. 14:8). The Promised Land turns out to be everything that they imagined and more. Spies report that there are clusters of grapes so large that it takes two men to carry them on a pole.

A few more centuries down the road, as the nation of Israel reaches its apex of wealth and influence under the rule of David's son, Solomon, we read of unprecedented wealth, wisdom, and global influence. Solomon's annual income in gold alone was worth, in today's standards, around $1.4 trillion a year.

When Revelation, the last book of the Bible, gives a description of heaven, and the place God has prepared for those who have trusted in Him, it is described as a place where the most valuable thing we can imagine on earth, gold, is simply the material used for pavement.

David would have been familiar with some of these; others were after his time. But the point is still the same. God is good! He demonstrates His goodness repeatedly in the bounty of creation in general, and in the love and grace and mercy He pours out on those who trust and follow Him. Spurgeon is right. When trauma and tragedy strike, and you cannot see where God is at work, trust His heart.

Victim Mentality?

One final word about choices: Trauma, sudden tragedy, and traumatic loss often involve circumstances in which someone is a victim. In other words, you suffered because of someone else's mistake, decision, negligence, or aggression. For many, once the trauma is past, the feeling of victimhood lingers on. A choice must be made here too. Post-traumatic growth often begins with a decision that the trauma you have suffered will not define who you are. But not making that choice is still a decision. It can be a passive decision to remain in a state of victimhood. I know sometimes it feels easiest to remain there. When people have experienced a trauma, they feel powerless; they feel like a victim. Something that they did not want to happen, happened anyway, and they were powerless to change the situation. They were victims. It is true. But to remain in the mindset of a victim is not necessary. As Frankl said, you can choose how you respond. My hope is this book gives you some tools and exercises to begin the move out of your victimhood and into healing.

Guided Reflection

Take a moment to reflect on the totality of Psalm 13. Reread it a few times and then use the following ideas to help you choose how you will move forward in the aftermath of your trauma.

1. Identify three things that continue to make you feel as though God has forgotten you.

2. Write a journal entry or talk to a friend about the specific ways that you wish that God would "restore the sparkle to your eyes."

3. Identify two ways in which you suspect others are "gloating" in your current circumstances. Ask yourself, "Are these valid feelings, responding to fact? Has someone actually blamed me for my current situation?" If so, you may want to seek out a trusted friend or counselor to help you determine if that blame is warranted or not. If not, perhaps it's time to let go of what others think or say.

4. As you think about choosing to trust God despite your current circumstances, which of the following resonates with you the most?

- God's unfailing love.

- The stories, from the Bible and other people, of times when God has rescued.
- The nature of God's goodness and bounty.

5. What is preventing you from choosing to trust God with your current situation?

6. Finally, perhaps with the help of a trusted friend or counselor, identify one thing related to your trauma that is keeping you in the role of the victim.

Chapter 7

New Normal

*"For I know the plans I have for you"—this is the
L*ORD*'s declaration—"plans for your well-being,
not for disaster, to give you a future and a hope."*
Jeremiah 29:11

THE NEW NORMAL. WHAT DOES that mean? The phrase became routine in 2020 as the COVID-19 pandemic wore into its first several months. Lockdowns were getting old and everyone seemed to be asking, "When will things get back to normal?" The response was, "Maybe we need to think of this as our new normal." The phrase and the idea of a "new normal," however, are not new. FBI Chaplain Joe Williams, who supervised pastoral care at the site of the 1995 bombing of the Oklahoma City Federal Building, introduced me to the concept of new normal in much of his work with grieving families. He said that any time we experience a loss, we must adjust to a new normal of life without the one who is gone. One way to understand grief is as a process of finding a new normal while adjusting to a loss.

In 1970, Elisabeth Kübler-Ross introduced her five stages of grief, or "five stages of death," as they were initially called:

(1) denial and isolation, (2) anger, (3) bargaining, (4) depression, and (5) acceptance.[22] These stages have been expanded and described differently by others. But in writing, Kübler-Ross helped us understand the concept of "new normal," even though she used different terms. She enunciated a process, the feelings and emotions that human beings go through when we experience deep loss. At first, we cannot believe something has happened. We just cannot wrap our minds around the feelings following an event of traumatic or sudden loss. I remember when one mother, upon arriving at the emergency room, discovered her son had been killed in a car accident. She couldn't accept that the teen to whom she said goodbye an hour earlier, on his way to work, was gone. She kept repeating that she had just seen him; it was impossible that he was dead.

Anger, depression, and isolation inevitably follow. But so does bargaining, which is where we often get stuck. People often believe, if only they had done [fill-in-the-blank] differently, their loved one would still be alive. They plead, often with God, to reverse the loss. They may cry, "God, take me instead! My son cannot be dead! Take me! Don't let this be!" What often follows is years of reliving the situation, trying to think of anything, any way, the loss could have been prevented. We all struggle to adjust to our new normal when tragedy strikes. We don't want to adjust. We deny what has happened, we bargain, we get angry at ourselves and the people around us. We get angry at God, and sometimes we are just mad at the world! In the best of circumstances, we slowly adjust as we accept the loss. In the worst, we sink into depression.

Ancient Israel found themselves in such a situation in 586 BC. Warnings from God to repent and turn from their evil ways persisted for around 150 years but were ignored. Finally, God allowed Babylon to invade and carry most of the population of Israel into captivity. The people who survived found themselves in Babylon and were in mourning. They desired to go home and get their old lives back. They struggled to adjust. Some were making plans to try to get back to Jerusalem. God sent this message to them through the prophet Jeremiah:

> This is what the LORD of Armies, the God of Israel, says to all the exiles I deported from Jerusalem to Babylon: "Build houses and live in them. Plant gardens and eat their produce. Find wives for yourselves, and have sons and daughters. Find wives for your sons and give your daughters to men in marriage so that they may bear sons and daughters. Multiply there; do not decrease. Pursue the well-being of the city I have deported you to. Pray to the LORD on its behalf, for when it thrives, you will thrive."
>
> For this is what the LORD of Armies, the God of Israel, says: "Don't let your prophets who are among you and your diviners deceive you, and don't listen to the dreams you elicit from them, for they are prophesying falsely to you in my name. I have not sent them." This is the LORD's declaration.

For this is what the LORD says: "When seventy years for Babylon are complete, I will attend to you and will confirm my promise concerning you to restore you to this place. For I know the plans I have for you"—this is the LORD's declaration—"plans for your well-being, not for disaster, to give you a future and a hope. You will call to me and come and pray to me, and I will listen to you. You will seek me and find me when you search for me with all your heart. I will be found by you"—this is the LORD's declaration—"and I will restore your fortunes and gather you from all the nations and places where I banished you"—this is the LORD's declaration. "I will restore you to the place from which I deported you." (Jer. 29:4–14)

As the Israeli captives were reeling from all that just happened, they found themselves in a foreign city, hundreds of miles away from anything familiar, longing for the lives that they had lost. They wanted life to get back to normal. God's message through Jeremiah the prophet might be paraphrased bluntly: "This is your new normal. Get used to it." God told the people to carry on with life—don't let life stop. He also warned them not to try to go back to their homeland. Then He gave them a time frame for how long their captivity would last. Finally, He assured them that He still had plans for their people. Much of modern, Western Christianity wants to skip to the promise without hearing the previous context and direction about how to live in the meantime. Jeremiah 29:11, the "plans I have for you" verse, is one of the most familiar and often quoted verses in American church culture. But we could learn much about how to grieve, about how to deal with trauma and loss, by pausing and reflecting on the context of this beloved passage.

Don't Try to Go Back

Our first instinct in such times is to try to put things back the way they were. We want to turn back time. In the aftermath of trauma or sudden loss, our natural inclination is to deny what has happened and go back to a time before the event took place. Kübler-Ross describes this instinct as part of the stage of denial. Simply put, we cannot deal with the reality of what happened, so in order to try to make sense of the world, our minds continually try to go back—to turn back time and live in a world before the tragedy. Denial is a normal and natural part of the grieving processes, but it is not helpful to remain there. While we all want to go back to a time before tragedy struck, we must face the fact that something unwanted happened and try to move on. Letting denial reign only delays the grief and recovery process. It also keeps us from shifting into full and vibrant lives in the present.

When Israel was carried away in exile to Babylon, the first instinct of many was to go back. Many of the other prophets seemed to be encouraging the people to go back and fight. God told the people through Jeremiah:

"Don't let your prophets who are among you and your diviners deceive you, and don't listen to the dreams you elicit from them, for they are prophesying falsely to you in my name. I have not sent them." (29:8)

God's message was very simply: "Don't go back."

In the case of loss, particularly traumatic loss, going back is not possible. The trauma occurred, and it cannot be undone. Yet we try to go back; we go back in our minds to the time before the traumatic event or loss. We often fall into a cycle of saying to ourselves and others, "If only I had been there; if only I acted differently; if only I hadn't said that; if only . . ." I call this the "coulda—woulda—shoulda game." In reality, it is no game. Here's what I mean: A trauma survivor says to themself there is something they could have done, should have done, or would have done differently. Knowing what they know now, they think they could have prevented the event. They beat themselves up, thinking that they should have acted differently, but those thoughts are dependent on knowledge they only have after the fact. Often the inner tension develops to a state that it creates such psychological turmoil that PTSD and, particularly, moral injury develop.

One Iraq war veteran lived every day with the knowledge that he had caused the death of someone who was innocent. In reality, there was nothing that he could have done differently. Many of his leaders assured him that he had done what was necessary in his responsibility to protect those around him. Yet, day after day, months after returning home, he continued to go back in his mind to find a way he could have prevented what happened.

In reality, there is no way to go back. That's true no matter what type of trauma, accident, abuse, or natural disaster has happened. When we wrestle with ourselves, trying to convince ourselves we could have acted differently, we create such a psychological tension that we find ourselves suffering from mental health disorders. As humans, we are subject to the reality of time. The only direction we can move is forward, toward acceptance of what has happened.

Carry On with Life

So how do you move forward? When bad things happen, life seems to stop. Nothing else matters. The trauma or loss we experience is all we can think about. Yet life goes on. Often, when people are grieving such intense and sudden losses, it is easy to let life slide away. One day becomes the same as the next. Depression sets in. There is an existence, but how could you call it living, let alone thriving? That is exactly where ancient Israel was. They were reeling from the devastation. They couldn't conceive of anything but how the only lives they had ever known were gone. They were in this mindset when Jeremiah's message came. One of the first things God said to them through the prophet was, essentially, "Get on with living." Jeremiah provided a kind of how-to list for moving forward: First, he said, "Build houses and live in them" (v. 5a). In other words, their first order of business was to settle into their new living arrangements. But it was more than just settling in, as if moving into an apartment. He said, "Build houses." Buying a house in a new community communicates that you expect to be there for a while, but *building* a house communicates an expectation of some permanence. They were told to build—to settle in and accept that this was their new home.

Second, the exiles were instructed to "plant gardens and eat their produce" (v. 5b). Planting gardens and eating their produce communicated another level of permanence related to the new living arrangements. It gave them something to do to keep busy, but it also forced them to think about practical things, like providing for their needs. It also helped to create a sense of normalcy—of getting back to doing the kinds of things they were used to in their agricultural society.

One lady told me after experiencing a sudden and significant loss that going back to work helped her adjust. She said, "If I just stay at home and think about it, I will go crazy. I need to get my mind off of it." For her, the routine of going back to work helped her reestablish what normal felt like. It also met the practical need of providing the financial resources on which she depended. In fact, for most people, staying home to grieve and sink into depression is not an option. They need to continue making a living.

Third, the people were told, "Find wives for yourselves, and have sons and daughters. Find wives for your sons and give your daughters to men in marriage so that they may bear sons and daughters" (v. 6a). The instructions were similar to our cultural expectations to settle down, get married, and start a family. The instructions were clear: "Multiply there; do not decrease" (v. 6b). Their families were expected to grow, develop, and thrive. In times of grief, it is easy to forget about others. Yet it is critically important to not just continue to connect with loved ones, but to also develop new friendships and relationships. One of the signs that people are starting to move on from a time of grief is that they start meeting new people again.

Last, they were to "pursue the well-being of the city I have deported you to. Pray to the LORD on its behalf, for when it thrives, you will thrive" (v. 7). In other words, they were to get involved in their communities, active in civic organizations, and work for the betterment of all. Their future well-being was tied to the well-being of the community in which they now lived.

By this point, you may have noticed that much of Jeremiah's instruction harmonizes with parts of Maslow's hierarchy of human needs we discussed in chapter 4. Each of these activities was meant to help Israel accept their new situation. Each carried with it a new connotation that indicated an increasing level of permanence in their circumstances. These instructions were meant to help the people begin to carry on with their new lives. The goal was not only to adapt in the short term, but thrive in their new homelands for the long term.

Over the course of a twenty-year military career, my wife and I often found ourselves feeling as though we were not fully living in a house, knowing that it was temporary. For example, throughout my career, we were registered to vote in our home state, we registered our vehicles at my parents' address, and we paid taxes according to where I entered the service. Everything seemed temporary, all the time. We knew that each assignment would only last two to three years, so we lived as though everything was transitory. What that meant was that we often missed out on *actually* living and enjoying all that each location had to offer.

When people experience sudden and traumatic loss of some kind, they sometimes hesitate to adjust to their new normal. Getting to what Kübler-Ross describes as acceptance involves moving out of a mentality that everything in life is temporary, transitory, or unpredictable. Thriving means that we must engage with life again. This means doing the kinds of things the Israelites were told to do in exile: Build a house, find a way to feed and take care of yourselves, pursue new relationships and establish new family ties, and get involved in your community to help others. Such activities are an indication that life is moving forward. Collectively, they build momentum for healing.

This Is Going to Take a While

Adjusting to a new normal, moving on with life after sudden or traumatic loss, takes time. But time is the last thing we want to think about during those moments, isn't it? We just want things to get back to normal. In the early days of the COVID-19 pandemic, some people said that COVID-19 would likely be with us for a couple of years. Others went further and said that we would have to live with it from now on. That was the last thing that people wanted to hear after two to three weeks of initial lockdowns. Yet much of the grieving process, as Kübler-Ross describes it, is about coming to terms with our losses—realizing that what we had hoped for is gone, and in its place is an alternate future that we never expected and certainly never wanted.

After God, through the prophet Jeremiah, tells the exiles to carry on with life, He then goes one step further. He says: "When seventy years for Babylon are complete, I will attend to you and will confirm my promise concerning you to restore you to this place" (v. 10). The message is simple: Israel will be exiled in Babylon for seventy years. No one will go back to the Promised Land or to Jerusalem until seven decades have passed. That was certainly an alternate future that no one in Israel wanted.

One of the most difficult experiences of my life was saying goodbye to my family as I prepared to depart for a seven-month deployment to Iraq with Marine Corps ground forces. The years 2005 and 2006 had been especially tough in Iraq, and early 2007 seemed no different as we completed pre-deployment training. Our departure time was late at night. My wife and kids dropped me off around 10:00 p.m. We gave long hugs, knowing that we would not see one another for seven months. The unspoken "elephant in the room" was the knowledge that it was war, and anything could happen. As I walked toward the headquarters building to check in, the door of the minivan swung open, and my daughter shrieked, "Daddy!!!" She ran toward me with one of the two old dog tags I had given her to keep for me. We hugged again, and she returned to the van, where I could see my wife in tears behind the driver's seat. As I walked into the building, everything within me screamed out to turn around and go back to be with them. In that moment, seven months felt like an eternity.

Whether it is seven months, seventy years, or a lifetime, adjustment to the reality of a new normal is hard. It takes time to accept what happened, and it takes time to realize the new way things are going to be. There is a misconception in modern culture, particularly among driven type A males, regarding grief. On more than one occasion, leaders have said to me, "I don't understand. We gave him leave time to go home for the funeral. We let him go talk to the chaplain. Why is he still having problems?" Such a mentality denies the most fundamental part of grief and traumatic grief—it takes time. The idea that everything should get back to normal and people should just be able to carry on after the funeral is over is not realistic. I like to describe it this way: If a person was in your life for twenty years, it is unlikely that you are going to be able to adjust to their absence in your life in twenty days. To think otherwise is ludicrous.

As the people of Israel grieved the loss of their homeland and their situation in exile, God was very clear with them: This is going to take seventy years. We would do better to be honest with survivors of trauma and loss as they are grieving. We should help set their expectations that grief takes a long time. Depending on the loss, it may take a year, ten years, or it may be something that you carry with you for a lifetime and never fully get over. But honest and realistic expectations (more about that in the next chapter) will challenge our culture that demands instant results for everything. So often we see normal grief as a problem to check off on a to-do list. But grief takes time.

I Still Have Plans for You

It is not until God helps Israel understand and adjust to their current living environment that He talks about future plans and promises. But notice that He does! God does not simply say, "Adjust; this is your new life. Sucks to be you." Look again at what He says: "For I know the plans I have for you," declares the Lord, "plans to prosper you and not to harm you, plans to give you hope and a future" (v. 11 NIV). The reality is that no matter how severe the trauma, grief, and loss, it is never the end of the story.

God could have told the Israelites, "I sent you prophets to warn you for 150 years, but you didn't listen, so now here is your future. Good luck with it." But that is not what God said to them. After telling them to settle in and adjust to their new circumstances, He reminded them that He still had plans for them.

There is a time and a place to talk about future hope and God's plans. Some people think that the way to provide comfort in the immediate aftermath of loss is to quote such Bible verses about the future. That is not what Jeremiah does. His message is first about helping the people to adjust to their new circumstances. It is only after the people are given instructions about accepting and adapting their current state of affairs that Jeremiah talks about the future. The future God describes to the people includes hope for what is to come. It also includes a discussion about their prosperity.

Prosperity

The prosperity described here does not refer to the modern understanding of prosperity in the sense of wealth and riches. Instead, prosperity here refers to the bigger picture of what it means to prosper—to grow and thrive in the world. Many people today talk about "well-being." Well-being more aptly describes what this passage is about. A state of well-being involves physical, mental, spiritual, emotional, and yes, even financial wellness. So, when God tells the captive Israelites that their future involves a time when they will again prosper, He is communicating His holistic care for them.

God really does care about your well-being. He has the best in mind for you. Consider what Jesus said to His followers about how God longs to care for His people:

> "Which of you, if your son asks for bread, will give him a stone? Or if he asks for a fish, will give him a snake? If you, then, though you are evil, know how to give good gifts to your children, how much more will your Father in heaven give good gifts to those who ask him!" (Matt. 7:9–11 NIV)

When traumatic events strike, some people think that God enjoys punishing them and taking away the things most precious to them. While traumatic events are a reality of our world, nothing could be further from the truth about God's desire. God wants a relationship with you and has your ultimate good and well-being in mind. He truly wants to see you grow and thrive again after your traumatic experience. God has not forsaken you. He gives good gifts to those who ask.

Think about it like this. A few months ago, I took my grandson to get his very first ice cream cone. He was not quite a year old at the time, and it was incredibly fun to watch him taste it—to see him try to understand the texture and the cold. Nothing makes me happier than caring for my three children and two grandchildren, giving them what they need to grow, develop, and flourish. When one of them is hurt, I do my best to help them find healing whether that is physical, mental, or emotional healing. If it is fulfilling to me as a father and grandfather to watch them grow and thrive, imagine what joy God must take in seeing His people prosper.

God told Israel that His plans included His people thriving again after what they had gone through. Thriving meant that they would first have to adjust to life in Babylon, settling into their new normal by doing all the things described so far in this chapter. But there was also a future quality about thriving. God told the people that they would prosper again.

The stage of grief that Kübler-Ross describes as acceptance includes coming to grips with our new normal in the aftermath of trauma. But acceptance is more than that. Acceptance also means that we are once again thriving, living a full life that includes enjoying all that life has to offer. That means enjoying the good things that God has given you. It also includes the ability to, once again, think about and plan for the future.

Hope and Future

Grief steals our ability to think beyond the present moment. We are consumed with the here and now, and the difficulty of adjusting to new circumstances. Trauma robs us of the ability to think about the future. As mentioned in chapter 4, Duncan Sinclair has said that one of the losses people experience as a result of PTSD is what he describes as the "Loss of Future."[23] Israel was certainly traumatized by their military defeat and subsequent exile to Babylon. But as God told the people to accept their new normal, He also reminded them that He still had future plans for them.

What must that have been like? After years of warnings from God, war with their captors, the long journey to a strange land, and the struggle to settle into their new lives, God then said, "I still have plans for you." It must have seemed like a breath of fresh air after all they had experienced—to hear that God still had plans for a future for them.

Acceptance of grief and trauma begins when we can once again think about life beyond the circumstances of what has happened or what has been lost. In May 2021, just as the Centers for Disease Control and Prevention (CDC) released its recommendations that it was alright for people to gather in groups again following the COVID-19 pandemic lockdowns and restrictions, Wrigley's Extra—the chewing gum—featured a television commercial that depicts people racing back to public places. They are seen running from apartment complexes, getting into dust-covered cars in the driveways of their homes, and moving in a hurried frenzy to parks, office buildings, and literally any public place where they can gather with other people again. The soundtrack for the commercial features Céline Dion's 1996 rendition of "It's All Coming Back to Me Now." Even a commercial for a simple product like chewing gum touched the emotions so many people felt at the time—the desire to step into the future and experience some type of normalcy again. There was hope that, after more than a year of isolation, people could begin to think about life beyond the pandemic and have hope for the future. Because there was hope, acceptance of all that had happened finally dawned.

Grief and loss make it difficult to think about the future. It can seem impossible to see beyond the circumstances of the present. So, when a glimmer of hope for the future finally comes, it changes everything. Such was the case for Israel. They had heard the message to settle into their new normal. But at the precise moment when they needed to hear of God's future plans, the prophet Jeremiah delivered hope. Whatever tragedy you have lived through, no matter how severe the trauma may have been, you still have a future ahead of you. Acceptance of your losses can be excruciating. The journey toward such acceptance can take many twists and turns through the various phases of grief: denial, anger, depression, bargaining. Yet acceptance always means coming to grips with your new reality and reordering life to the new normal. God's redemptive hand is still at work in your situation. It is His desire that you once again thrive in life. Just as God still had plans for a future for the people of Israel, it is His desire that you know that He still has plans for your life as well. There is a still a future out there for you!

Guided Reflection

Take a moment and reflect on the various messages that God gave to Israel through the prophet Jeremiah. What stands out to you the most?

Now, circle the following actions you need to take given your present reality:

1. I need to stop going back in my mind to try to change what happened. I need to accept that I cannot change what has happened.

2. I need to figure out the right living situation for me now. Specifically, which of these fits me?

- I need to sell my house and make a fresh start.
- I need to move in with family for support.
- I need to separate from family who are keeping me from moving on with life.
- I need to get an apartment.
- I need to either go back to work or get a job so that I have something to keep my mind occupied.

3. I need to figure out my relationships.

- I need to try to make some new friends or reconnect with old friends.

- I need to be more involved in the lives of my children, grandchildren, or other family members.
- I need to start dating again.

4. I need to get involved in my community or church in order to provide me with purpose and also give back.

5. I need to thank God that He has not forgotten me.

6. I need to realize that God still wants me to thrive in life—that He still has a future for me.

Chapter 8

Expectations

*"In this world you will have trouble. But
take heart! I have overcome the world."*
John 16:33b NIV

"IT'S NOT SUPPOSED TO BE this way!" I have heard those words uttered so often, by a grieving husband who thought he would die before his wife, from the lips of a mother who lost her only child, from a father just notified that his son was killed in war, from a young sailor whose mother died just after he reported to boot camp, and a host of others. To say, "It's not supposed to be this way," means we expected life to be something other than what we experienced. Most of us in the Western world expect life to be healthy, happy, and prosperous. We may not say that out loud, but deep down we expect we will achieve our dreams and "live happily ever after." But life is not that way. We experience death, divorce, disease, disaster, and dozens of other losses natural to life on earth. All too often our expectations about what life will look like are not realistic.

But what does it mean to have realistic expectations of life? A quick internet search of the phrase *realistic expectations* nets a myriad of results including YouTube videos, multiple mental health and self-help websites, and even a Shutterstock page with more than five hundred images purportedly related to the topic. It's true, having realistic expectations in life is important. Realistic expectations help us to manage our emotions. For example, employers routinely recommend that supervisors set realistic expectations about working hours, pay, promotion opportunities, and a multitude of other things. Mental health professionals assist their clients in readjusting expectations related to relationships with significant others, and financial advisors help customers to have realistic expectations about the growth of their money and how far it may go in retirement.

For all the talk about realistic expectations, though, many people still live with expectations of a happy, healthy, and care-free life. For many Americans in particular, a dream means a successful career, home ownership in a comfortable neighborhood near the best schools, a preferred number of children, and maybe a three-car garage. It also means a happy and healthy life, where everyone you love continues to grow, flourish, and thrive. There is often a surprising lack of realism about life and death. If life is relatively good, people seem to hold on to the idea that it will always be that way. There seems to be an unwritten rule that if you do all the "right things," life will go well for you, and you will never experience difficulty. Disease can be managed or even avoided by preventative health measures such as diet, exercise, and regular wellness exams. Accidents can be avoided by avoiding risky behaviors, unsafe areas, and doing things like driving responsibly. There are partial truths in those expectations, but they aren't guarantees.

Such expectations about life seem to be indelibly marked on our human psyche. In fact, Bill Nash, retired Navy psychologist, says it this way:

> . . . people also need to believe that they are safe—that their lives will not be snuffed out in the next few seconds—and that a moral order exists in the universe that discriminates right from wrong.[24]

The need for safety that Nash describes harmonizes with Maslow's hierarchy of human needs, discussed earlier, which emphasizes physical safety as a basic human need. But if you look closely at what Nash is saying, he goes on to say: ". . . that discriminates right from wrong." In other words, people not only need to feel that they are physically safe, in a moment, but they also need to believe that life makes sense from a moral perspective—that good happens to good people, and bad people receive the just rewards of their actions. What does not make sense for most of us is when bad things happen to good people, or bad people seem to prosper and go unpunished. Our innate sense of right and wrong just does not want to tolerate such a world. In fact, wherever we find such injustice, human beings have an innate desire to correct it, to root it out and destroy it. We want to set the world right.

When war, natural disaster, abuse, accidents, and disease remind us that the world is not safe, we question the moral order that Nash described. When we see the devastation of a hurricane, tornado, or tsunami destroying the lives of otherwise good people, we question that moral order. The violations of our desire for moral order and sense of safety can later result in the development of PTSD or moral injury symptoms, similar to the soldier or Marine who sees a buddy killed in combat, or the young woman raped on her college campus, or the wife whose husband dies in a car crash as she watches him take his last breath.

In a world where such a disconnect exists between our expectations and our lived experience, we tend to blame God, ourselves, or others for what has happened. But this kind of blame is useless. Such hurt and pain have been part of the human experience since the beginning of time. We live in a world filled with trauma, grief, and traumatic loss. Yet as Nash and Maslow remind us, we need to believe that we are safe, and we expect that we will never experience such tragedies. However, if we are going to have realistic expectations of life, we need to shift our expectations and stop expecting to be completely safe and secure on planet Earth. Rather than blaming God, ourselves, or others for things that happen, perhaps we should accept that it was never promised to us to live trouble-free lives in this world. In His last hours on earth, Jesus Christ gave His followers some perspective on this, saying:

> In this world you will have trouble. But take heart! I have overcome the world. (John 16:33b NIV)

Trouble

Although we should expect that trouble is a part of life, and that no one is immune to tragedy striking, most of us don't. In fact, the first question that often comes to mind when trauma hits, is "Why?" Up to this point, we've talked about the emotions behind the why. But it is worthwhile taking the time to ask the question, "Why does there have to be trouble in this world at all?" Jesus told His followers that they would have trouble in this world, that it is a part of life, and that they should expect it personally. But the question remains: Why do we have to experience trouble and hardship in this life in the first place? To find the answer to this question, we must go back in time, way back to the very beginning of human existence.

In the creation account of Genesis, we are told that God made everything and that it was very good! "God saw all that he had made, and it was very good" (Gen. 1:31a NIV). Yet less than seven hundred words later in the text, we read the following account:

> Now the serpent was more crafty than any of the wild animals the LORD God had made. He said to the woman, "Did God really say, 'You must not eat from any tree in the garden'?"
> The woman said to the serpent, "We may eat fruit from the trees in the garden, but God did say, 'You must not eat fruit from the tree that is in the middle of the garden, and you must not touch it, or you will die.'"

"You will not certainly die," the serpent said to the woman. "For God knows that when you eat from it your eyes will be opened, and you will be like God, knowing good and evil."

When the woman saw that the fruit of the tree was good for food and pleasing to the eye, and also desirable for gaining wisdom, she took some and ate it. She also gave some to her husband, who was with her, and he ate it. Then the eyes of both of them were opened, and they realized they were naked; so they sewed fig leaves together and made coverings for themselves.

Then the man and his wife heard the sound of the Lord God as he was walking in the garden in the cool of the day, and they hid from the Lord God among the trees of the garden. But the Lord God called to the man, "Where are you?"

He answered, "I heard you in the garden, and I was afraid because I was naked; so I hid."

And he said, "Who told you that you were naked? Have you eaten from the tree that I commanded you not to eat from?"

The man said, "The woman you put here with me—she gave me some fruit from the tree, and I ate it."

Then the LORD God said to the woman, "What is this you have done?"

The woman said, "The serpent deceived me, and I ate."

So the LORD God said to the serpent, "Because you have done this,

> "Cursed are you above all livestock
>   and all wild animals!
> You will crawl on your belly
>   and you will eat dust
>   all the days of your life.
> And I will put enmity
>   between you and the woman,
>   and between your offspring and hers;
> he will crush your head,
>   and you will strike his heel."

To the woman he said,

> "I will make your pains in childbearing
>   very severe;
>   with painful labor you will give birth
>   to children.
> Your desire will be for your husband,
>   and he will rule over you."

To Adam he said, "Because you listened to your wife and ate fruit from the tree about which I commanded you, 'You must not eat from it,'

> "Cursed is the ground because of you;
>   through painful toil you will eat food
>   from it
>   all the days of your life.
> It will produce thorns and thistles for you,
>   and you will eat the plants of the field.
> By the sweat of your brow
>   you will eat your food
> until you return to the ground,
>   since from it you were taken;
> for dust you are
>   and to dust you will return."
> (Gen. 3:1–19 NIV)

Prior to this, Adam and Eve lived in blissful harmony. We are not told how long this time of perfect serenity lasted. It could have been a few days, or it could have been many years. What we are told is how such perfect peace ended—it ended with the first traumatic event in human history, the direct defiance of the Creator God Himself. Here we are told of the results of such defiance, a curse inflicted upon not only humanity but the created order itself that resulted in physical pain, emotional distance, and spiritual isolation.

Each generation subsequently adds to the rebellion, in large and small ways, and in turn the curse's impact increases in both direct and indirect ways. One might argue this point, saying, "I never did anything to deserve COVID-19, or cancer, or . . ." While that may be true on one level, we all live in a world where, because of the curse of rebellion, it went from being a paradise to a planet whose very surface was cursed with thorns and thistles. The natural world no longer cooperates in such a way that food grows spontaneously without hard work. It is easy, then, to see how after generations and generations of degradation, new diseases arose as part of the curse and indirectly impact every individual on planet Earth, such as what happened with the COVID-19 pandemic and other previous ones. As the Genesis narrative continues in the chapters that follow, we read the first event of envy and jealousy that resulted in the first murder, until eventually full-blown wars developed. It all began with one little taste of forbidden fruit. One act of defiance led to another; one piece of the curse grew in both scope and consequences until, finally, Jesus told His disciples, we should also expect trouble.

History is filled with examples of trouble; few events are unique to the twentieth and twenty-first centuries. For example: The Bubonic plague took the lives of millions in Europe in the fourteenth century; the Roman Empire subjugated lands from India to Spain; Mongolian hordes spent one hundred years killing and conquering most of Asia; ancient Egypt used slave labor to build the pyramids; and famine and disease were repeatedly described in biblical times. The eruption of Mount Vesuvius in AD 79 buried Pompei and another nearby city in hot volcanic ash. The list could go on, but you get the idea.

The reality of life on planet Earth is that we all face challenging situations as part of daily living. In the modern era those challenges can take on many different forms like cancer, job loss, bankruptcy, pandemic, war, economic uncertainty, traffic accidents, natural disasters, sexual assault, and many more.

Suffering, trouble, and hardship have always been part of life. A professor of mine once said his one-word definition of life was "struggle." When Jesus told His followers that they would experience trouble, He meant it on both the macro and micro levels. That trouble will be on a grand scale, and trouble will find each of us individually. That is the difficult part of this. In the back of each of our minds, we can intellectually agree that all those things described at the beginning of the chapter are present in our world. What most of us do not expect is the likelihood of those things touching us individually.

For the eleven men to whom Jesus spoke on that night, church tradition tells us that all but one of them would die a violent death because they followed Him. Four were crucified. Peter was one of those, although he was crucified upside down. Two were stoned to death; one was speared. James was beheaded; Bartholomew was beaten, then crucified. John was the only one of them who died of old age, and even then, he was exiled to the island of Patmos. None of them went on to live a carefree life. When Jesus told them they would have trouble in this world, it was not an abstract concept to them; they each experienced it personally.

Ironically, the words of Jesus in the passage above were spoken the night before He was to be crucified. Jesus experienced hardship Himself. The evening began with Jesus washing His disciples' feet in a symbolic act of humility and service. Later they enjoyed the Passover Meal celebration and the Last Supper. Then Judas Iscariot left in the middle of the meal to betray Him. While Jesus knew all that was about to happen to Him, the

EXPECTATIONS

remaining eleven disciples did not. Although Jesus did tell them three times over the course of the pages leading up to the statement above that very soon He would no longer be with them. He told them that He was going to prepare a place for them, and that He would leave a comforter for them. But in the hours before He died on the cross, Jesus wanted to make sure that those who had followed Him were under no delusions; He wanted them to know that they would face difficulty in this present world.

Setting realistic expectations that life is, in fact, filled with trouble may be key to accepting the difficult things that ultimately become part of our lives. For example, during one period of geopolitical uncertainty, my ship was preparing to deploy. As was often the case before we set sail, my office was filled with young sailors describing personal situations and hardships related to the deployment. One young woman, with tears rolling down her cheeks, said, "I can't go to sea." Her situation was not unique and was certainly not very different from the hardships that others were enduring. So, I asked her about her expectations: Why had she joined the Navy? Had she considered that Navy ships went to sea for long periods of time? She responded, "No, sir. I just thought it was another branch of the service, and I could be stationed close to home." Obviously, her unrealistic expectations had not met with the reality of Naval service. While this story may be a bit humorous, the reality is that she had not counted the cost of joining the military. When the hardship of her commitment was upon her, she balked. Her story illustrates the point that many of us (though, not everyone) can intellectually grasp the idea that there is trouble in our world. We just do not want it to come our way! Jesus wanted His followers to be prepared for the hardships that would come their way. But by extension, I think He wants us all to understand that our ultimate hope can never be rooted in this world—because this world is full of trouble! The physical safety and moral order for which we long cannot ultimately be found on planet Earth.

That does not stop us from trying to fix everything though. Throughout history, human beings repeatedly attempted to restore peace and harmony on earth. Yet, every time we have tried to do so we have created new trauma rather than solving the results of the previous one. In the past one hundred years alone, world leaders, out of a resolve to never have another war like World War I, made decisions that resulted directly and indirectly in World War II, the Korean War, the Vietnam War, the Cold War, the unraveling of the Middle East, and the rise of terrorism and wars in Iraq and Afghanistan, along with a host of others. Communism, Nazism, Capitalism, Socialism, Liberalism, and Conservatism—all the "isms"—all purport to be the answer to the world's problems. They promise a utopia on earth that includes peace and prosperity. In the end, they all fail in doing so. That does not stop people from trying.

When speaking about moral injury and its many causes during a recent conference, one lecturer went so far as to say that we need to identify the things in our world that cause moral injury so that we can work to put a stop to them. In other words, human beings need to find the sources of trauma that are causing moral injury so that we can stop them. But as we have seen, that is not reality. As hard as we try to fix the world, all our answers are imperfect. In short, we lack the ability to fix all the ills of the world and restore the created order and the perfect paradise of Eden.

Blame

As a result, human beings long to affix blame. Somehow, people feel as though they are making things right by laying blame to a responsible party. We do this in several ways. First, we blame God for what has happened. As mentioned in previous chapters, people say that if God were all powerful, surely, He could have prevented the event from happening in the first place. As I shared in the early chapters of this book, there was one young Marine that I met in Iraq who would tolerate no talk about God. For him, the fact that we were in Iraq and that he had seen so much and lost so many of his buddies in previous deployments was proof positive that there could be no God. How could there be, when so much pain and tragedy was part of life? Instead, he saw religion as a crutch for the weak-minded rather than the source of hope. He was blaming God for all that had happened in his life and taking his frustration out on those who continued to believe.

Second, people blame others. We demand that someone be held accountable for the results of the traumatic event or tragedy. To restore the moral order described by Nash, we insist that someone be held accountable. Righteous indignation and moral "high-horsing" can often be part of this. This is on full display in modern cancel culture. Unfortunately, blaming others often ends with bitterness and angry resentment rather than any kind of positive outlook that might extend grace or forgiveness. The Korean War veteran, mentioned in chapter 1, still blamed the death of a friend on the incompetence of a leader more than sixty years later. His anger was apparent, although he was taking positive steps toward finding a resolution. For many though, such anger can be all-consuming, and the blame they seek to affix to others to make things right only consumes them from the inside.

Finally, people blame themselves when something bad happens. Blaming oneself for a traumatic event is just anger turned inward. It is the kind of anger and frustration that says, "I should have done something differently." It is the self-loathing and second-guessing that says, "If only I had known, I would have done something differently." Or the belief that, "I could have stopped it, if only . . ." What we don't realize here is that no amount of internal anger or rehashing of what happened will change things. Blaming God, others, or ourselves will never undo the trauma or change the fact that, in this world, we will, indeed, experience trouble.

Overcome

As much as we want to find safety and security, rest and restoration, in this life, it is to be found elsewhere. Jesus did not end His statement with: "In this world you will have trouble" (John 16:33b NIV), as if we should just accept that suffering is a part of life and get over it. That kind of thought process can be found in the nihilist philosophy that says there is no meaning in anything; nothing really matters in life. That is not where Jesus left us or His followers. He wanted us to know that He had defeated our pain and suffering, as well as the consequences of human rebellion. So, He continued by saying, "But take heart! I have overcome the world" (v. 33b).

When Jesus spoke these words, He had not yet died on the cross, nor had He risen from the dead. Over the next eighteen hours He experienced betrayal, abandonment, mockery, beating, and execution by the cruelest method ever devised. This was a bold statement, knowing the reality of the suffering that He was about to endure. From the way He spoke, it is as if He was saying that He had already accomplished His mission of restoration. As the eternal son of God, He could see beyond His temporal suffering to what it would accomplish. It was as if it had already been completed—because He could see the other side. Despite all that was going on around Him that night, though, Jesus focused on the other side of His crucifixion and all that it would accomplish. He wanted His followers to not only accept that they would have trouble in this world, but also to trust that He had everything under control.

The significance of those words in the context of what was about to happen to Jesus cannot be overstated. Christians believe that Jesus's death on the cross perfectly satisfied the requirements of a sacrificial Passover lamb as written in the Jewish Mosaic Law, that through His death and resurrection, Jesus overcame death itself and paid the penalty of sin for all of humanity for all time. In other words, the curse that was described in Genesis 3 was reversed because He satisfied the sacrificial requirements for humanity which lifted God's curse upon humanity and the entire created order.

That sounds great, but you are probably wondering, "What does that mean in the context of trouble, hardship, and trauma as they relate to realistic expectations of life?" Just as Jesus was able to see through His suffering and focus on what His death would accomplish, we can now also trust that God sees through our difficulties and hardships. Trauma is never the end of anyone's story. God's redemptive activity is at work even in the most tragic situations. This was true for Jesus's eleven remaining disciples as well. In those early hours after the crucifixion, they thought that the trauma of His public execution was the end of the story and the end of their hopes and dreams. They even feared that it might be the end of their lives as well. Yet His resurrection filled them with excitement and passion. It emboldened them to change the world within a century.

Jesus's statement also means that trauma need not define us. Trauma is something that happens to us; it is not part of who we are at our core. Sure, your traumatic memories will always be part of your life. You will live with them throughout your lifetime, and they can even shape your personality and the way that you look at the world. However, to say that trauma is just part of who you are is to surrender to it; to let it define you, rather than you integrating the experience into the overall tapestry of your life. One young Marine experienced significant hardship during his deployment to Iraq. His experiences, however, caused him to believe in God and commit his life to following Jesus Christ. He later became a Navy chaplain, serving other young Marines. The point is that God can use your traumatic experiences to prepare you to serve others.

Some people think that Jesus's statement is more of a pie-in-the-sky message; that trouble and hardship are part of this lifetime, but not present in the next. While that line of thinking has some truth in it, people can sometimes use it to justify ending their pain by suicide. Nothing in what has been said so far should lead to that conclusion. Pain is part of this lifetime, but it is not all that there is to this life. Even after trauma, there are still things to enjoy in this life. When Jesus says that He has overcome, He also means that He is at work in our lives in a redemptive way, bringing about something good from our pain. He can turn any story around. (More about that in chapter 9.)

Finally, when Jesus speaks of overcoming this world, He is also referring to the time when He will ultimately recreate the entire universe. Notice how one of the very last passages of the Bible describes it:

> Then I saw "a new heaven and a new earth," for the first heaven and the first earth had passed away, and there was no longer any sea. I saw the Holy City, the new Jerusalem, coming down out of heaven from God, prepared as a bride beautifully dressed for her husband. And I heard a loud voice from the throne saying, "Look! God's dwelling place is now among the people, and he will dwell with them. They will be his people, and God himself will be with

them and be their God. 'He will wipe every tear from their eyes. There will be no more death' or mourning or crying or pain, for the old order of things has passed away."

He who was seated on the throne said, "I am making everything new!" Then he said, "Write this down, for these words are trustworthy and true."

He said to me: "It is done. I am the Alpha and the Omega, the Beginning and the End. To the thirsty I will give water without cost from the spring of the water of life. Those who are victorious will inherit all this, and I will be their God and they will be my children." (Rev. 21:1–7 NIV)

Guided Reflection

As human beings, we should learn to expect that traumatic experiences, trouble, and hardship are part of human existence. Accepting that reality means that we cannot restore peace on earth through our own human wisdom or effort. It also means that we should avoid trying to find someone to blame when tragedy strikes. Ultimately, we must trust that God not only sees our pain, but He also overcame it! Consider the following questions as you reflect on Jesus's statement:

EXPECTATIONS

1. Is your first reaction when something bad happens to try to find someone to blame? If so, who? How could learning to extend grace and forgiveness change your outlook?

2. What might be some of your unrealistic expectations about trouble and hardship in life? For example: Do you assume that life should always make sense? Are you surprised when tragedy strikes you, as if you should be immune to the heartaches of life? How do you react when such things come into your life? What does this say about how you should adjust your outlook on life?

3. What does it mean to you to accept that Jesus has overcome your trauma?

Chapter 9

I Only Thought I Knew You

"He brought me up from a desolate pit . . ."
Psalm 40:2a

THE MIDWATCH. THE DARKEST TIME of the night, from midnight to 4:00 a.m. Sailors on every Navy ship remain vigilant throughout the night, watching for navigational hazards, other vessels, hostile forces, and those in distress at sea. In doing so, they fight boredom and their own circadian rhythms to ensure the safety and security of their crew. This requires coffee with a viscosity akin to motor oil and the grit and determination to stay alert and serve while others sleep peacefully. But the midwatch can seem long and feel as though it drags on with no end through the midnight hours.

Such is the experience of those who endure the aftermath of trauma, grief, and traumatic loss. The trauma occurs suddenly, without warning. But the aftermath takes the lives of those who are precious and leaves its victim in an emotional and psychological darkness that seems to go on without end. Sometimes months and even years pass while those who suffer sink into pits of darkness, depression, grief, and sometimes PTSD or even moral injury.

But just as dawn follows every midwatch, so there is a time for the trauma victim when glimmers of hope begin to overtake what has been dark and hopeless for so long. For every dark night, there is a dawn; for every traumatic loss there is a moment when life can be renewed, even transformed to the point that life can seem normal again. For all the questions to God—"Why has this happened?" and "Where are you?"—there can be glimmers of faith and hope that spark the dawning realization that God, who was thought to be absent, has been there all the time. He is the one who ultimately cared the most about your pain and loss. It was God who was with you in the darkest moments of your life; He was there in the pit of despair, and often was the only one there. It is only when such an epiphany occurs that you finally realize that you have come to know God in a way that you only thought you knew before trauma struck—a God who rescues, who gave you the patience to endure the darkness and confusion, and who puts a song in your heart and on your lips again.

The writer of Psalm 40, whom we again believe to be King David, describes his experience of waiting for the Lord and the newness that God ultimately brought in his life:

> I waited patiently for the LORD,
> and he turned to me and heard my cry for
> > help.
> He brought me up from a desolate pit,
> out of the muddy clay,

and set my feet on a rock,
making my steps secure.
He put a new song in my mouth,
a hymn of praise to our God.
Many will see and fear,
and they will trust in the Lord. (vv. 1–3)

God Rescues

After multiple times of running for his life, hiding from those trying to kill him, and feeling abandoned by the God he served, David said in Psalm 40 that God "heard my cry for help" (v. 1) and "brought me up from a desolate pit, out of the muddy clay, and set my feet on a rock, making my steps secure" (v. 2). Survivors of trauma, grief, and traumatic loss understand very well what David meant by the term *desolate pit*. Anyone who has lived through the horrors of trauma can describe in detail their own pit, and what that experience was like. David lived this too. There were multiple occasions when his life was threatened: He faced Goliath, a nine-foot giant with only a slingshot; his predecessor and father-in-law later became jealous of his military feats and on at least two occasions tried to pin him to a wall with a javelin; and Saul hunted David down as he attempted to hide in the wilderness. After David became king, his own son Absalom led a revolt, and David again fled for his life. The revolt was squashed, and Absalom was killed. As we have seen, David composed many psalms of lament to mark these occasions. His cry was often, "God, why? God, where are you? God, how long?" Sound familiar?

Yet on each occasion, God rescued David. Afterward he was able to look back and say as he wrote the words of Psalm 40: "[The Lord] heard my cry for help [and] brought me up from a desolate pit, out of the muddy clay, and set my feet on a rock, making my steps secure" (vv. 1b–2).

Such a change in perspective reminds me of another man who experienced what David described as life in a "desolate pit." His name was Job, and his story is found in the Bible in a book named after him. Job was an extremely wealthy and influential guy. Notice how he is described:

> In the land of Uz there lived a man whose name was Job. This man was blameless and upright; he feared God and shunned evil. He had seven sons and three daughters, and he owned seven thousand sheep, three thousand camels, five hundred yoke of oxen and five hundred donkeys, and had a large number of servants. He was the greatest man among all the people of the East.
>
> His sons used to hold feasts in their homes on their birthdays, and they would invite their three sisters to eat and drink with them. When a period of feasting had run its course, Job would make arrangements for them to be purified. Early in the morning he would sacrifice a burnt

offering for each of them, thinking, "Perhaps my children have sinned and cursed God in their hearts." This was Job's regular custom. (Job 1:1–5 NIV)

Job's practices were well known in his community. He was doing everything right according to the customs of his day and, as a result, he prospered. We would describe him like this today: he owned his own businesses, he was worth a fortune, he was a great father and family man, he was a pillar of the community, and he was a man of deep faith who gave generously to charity. Who doesn't want to see someone like that do well? Then out of the blue, he lost everything. All ten of his children, his wealth, his possessions, and even his reputation were gone in one day. Read the description of what happened:

> One day when Job's sons and daughters were feasting and drinking wine at the oldest brother's house, a messenger came to Job and said, "The oxen were plowing and the donkeys were grazing nearby, and the Sabeans attacked and made off with them. They put the servants to the sword, and I am the only one who has escaped to tell you!"
>
> While he was still speaking, another messenger came and said, "The fire of God fell from the heavens and burned up the sheep and the servants, and I am the only one who has escaped to tell you!"

> While he was still speaking, another messenger came and said, "The Chaldeans formed three raiding parties and swept down on your camels and made off with them. They put the servants to the sword, and I am the only one who has escaped to tell you!"
>
> While he was still speaking, yet another messenger came and said, "Your sons and daughters were feasting and drinking wine at the oldest brother's house, when suddenly a mighty wind swept in from the desert and struck the four corners of the house. It collapsed on them and they are dead, and I am the only one who has escaped to tell you!"
>
> At this, Job got up and tore his robe and shaved his head. (vv. 13–20a NIV)

Job experienced unimaginable loss. His family and everything he had worked for throughout his lifetime were gone in an instant. If that was not enough, shortly thereafter, his health began to fail as well. A number of Job's friends showed up to comfort him in his grief, but ultimately, they added to his pain by suggesting that his losses were his own fault. They opined that there must be some evil deed that he had done, some secret intrigue that he had planned and carried out; now he must pay the consequences. Job insisted upon his innocence, even as their pressure rose, insisting upon his guilt. Like David, Job questioned God. He wondered why all this happened to him when he had been playing life by the rules—when he had been faithful to God and had cared for the poor and needy in his community—when he had never wronged anyone. As Job cried out to God in heart-wrenching lament, he begged God for a hearing to understand why he was going through such dark and difficult times. Like us, Job and his friends believed that people who are "living right" should not experience loss and tragedy, and that those who do, must have done something wrong.

Years ago, I knew a man who was involved in a large truck accident. When he awoke in the hospital, he said to the staff, "I must have done something wrong; otherwise, this would not have happened." We want to believe that good things happen to good people and bad things happen to bad people. Like Job, his friends, and the man I knew, our worlds are rocked when bad things happen to good people. It doesn't make sense and we long to make sense of our tragedies.

As Job cried out to hear from God, to try to make sense of things, his friends said he would never hear from God—that Job must simply acknowledge what he had done wrong. Things got heated. Loving friends, who had come to provide support, turned adversarial. Their accusations became hurtful. Just at the point when it seemed as though the darkness would go on forever, God spoke. God appeared to Job and his friends. He dismissed the theories that Job's suffering had been his own fault, challenged Job and his friends to realize that they never have the full picture as God does, and then restored Job's fortunes twofold. He also blessed him with another ten children. After all the questions, after all the wondering why such pain and darkness had come upon him, listen to Job's reaction to God:

> "I know that you can do all things;
> > no purpose of yours can be thwarted.
>
> You asked, 'Who is this that obscures my plans
> > without knowledge?'
> > Surely I spoke of things I did not
> > understand,
>
> things too wonderful for me to know.
>
> "You said, 'Listen now, and I will speak;
> > I will question you,
> > and you shall answer me.'
> > **My ears had heard of you**
> > **but now my eyes have seen you.**
> > Therefore I despise myself
> > > and repent in dust and ashes." (Job
> > > 42:2–6 NIV, emphasis added)

It is as if Job said to God, "I only thought that I knew You before I went through all of this. I had heard about You, I had even believed in You, but now I really know that You are the God who was with me all along, who knew what I was going through, and who ultimately rescued me from the pit that I was in!" Although there were no answers to Job's questions of "Why?" he had a new understanding and appreciation for God's love, compassion, and infinite wisdom. It was as if the experience had breathed a new awareness of God into Job's life. He was able to look at life through a fresh perspective and see God's love and wisdom as broader than he had ever imagined.

Like many of us, Job believed in God before trauma struck, but his relationship with God was untested. It combined an intellectual assent with dutiful obedience. When tragedy struck, such a faith was insufficient; he questioned everything that he thought that he knew about God, and in turn, his friends questioned his integrity. Through the experience, though, Job found a new and deeper faith. It was a faith in God that accepted that we may never understand why we experienced trauma, grief, and loss; a faith that is not a mathematical formula that says that if we do good, God is obligated to bless us. Job experienced a richer and more intimate relationship with God than he had ever imagined was possible before trauma and loss. Afterward, the world made sense in a whole new way! Old Testament scholar Walter Brueggemann describes such experiences like this:

> But the reality of the new experience is something other than, and more than what can be caught in and confined. . . . It is the experience that the world has a new coherence, that the devastating hopelessness of the lament is not finally appropriate for the way life is.[25]

A new outlook on life, a vibrant freshness and vitality to life, is what David was talking about in Psalm 40 when he said, "He turned to me and heard my cry for help. He brought me up from a desolate pit, out of the muddy clay, and set my feet on a rock, making my steps secure" (vv. 1b–2). God heard Job; He rescued him and gave him a new and stable life! He did the same for David, and He continues to do the same for people today. The pit of trauma and despair is never the end of the story. God wants us to know His presence in our trauma.

As I mentioned in chapter 4, an Afghan war veteran came home with a traumatic brain injury. He struggled for several years to function, and his symptoms caused significant problems with his family. Finally, he sought help and found doctors who could provide the appropriate medications to manage his symptoms. Today, when he speaks about the experience, however, he talks about how his faith in God is what brought him and his family through the difficulties of that experience. He said that he always believed in God, but it wasn't until he experienced the challenges of his injuries and their impact upon his family that he felt like he really knew what it meant to have a relationship with God—to be rescued by God. For this man, life and faith in God made sense in a new way after his injuries that would never have happened had he not gone through what he did.

Notice, though, that Job's questions remained. While the narrative of Job's story includes the cosmic reasons for his suffering, Job himself never discovered them. He lived the rest of his life with the loss of his children. While Job was able to move on and experience God's rescue and reward, he also continued to live with the grief of those losses. New life does not mean that we forget what was lost. Instead, we integrate those losses in such a way that, as Brueggemann said earlier, life has a new coherence. But that takes time.

For Job, for David, and for us, it means going through the pits of life and discovering that God is there even in the darkest times, and that He rescues us from those pits and helps us to have a new life that makes sense in a whole new way. Traumatic experiences are a part of life. They always have been, and they always will be.[26] Trauma brings grief and loss that are lifelong. God's redemptive activity in our lives brings us up out of the pits that we experience as a result of trauma and helps us to understand life from a new perspective—a perspective that helps us to learn and grow, to accept that life can make sense in a new way in the aftermath of trauma and that we can have a richer understanding of God, and of life, because of what we have experienced.

Rescue looks different for everyone. For some people, it is dramatic and involves an epiphany of some kind. Maybe it requires some radical readjustment to a new life such as moving to a different city, changing careers, getting remarried, or deciding to have another child. For others, rescue can simply mean learning to appreciate again all that life has to offer.

Patience

Notice, though, that for David and for Job, such a new understanding of life did not happen in an instant. In fact, it took a long time. David was on the run for years, and on multiple occasions, in his life. We are not told how long Job's experience lasted, but the text hints that it was a significant period. For many veterans that I have worked with, the pain and darkness went on for years before they began to experience hope again in their lives. Notice how David describes in Psalm 40 what it was like for him during these years: "I waited patiently for the Lord, and he turned to me and heard my cry for help" (v. 1).

We've all heard the statement, "Waiting is the hardest part!" Whether it is waiting for the results of medical tests or waiting to hear from a prospective employer, waiting is hard. Perhaps the hardest wait of all is in the aftermath of traumatic loss, when it seems as though things are never going to be different. It often seems that the pain and darkness will always be there. Trauma, grief, and loss require us to wait. They require us to stop and adjust emotionally, spiritually, and sometimes physically, before we can move on. For many who experience PTSD or moral injury, part of the problem is that life does move on, and it can seem as though life has moved on without them.

Despite being on the run, feeling threatened and abandoned, David said that he waited patiently for the Lord. Patience does not come naturally during the best times of life, let alone after a traumatic event. In fact, I'm not sure that I have ever waited patiently. When I am on the telephone and holding for a customer service agent, the familiar recording that says, "Thank you for your patience," usually irritates me and is a reminder that I am not a very patient person. During difficult periods of my life, when I am waiting on God to intervene in a matter I have been praying about, I often say things like, "God, I don't understand. God, where are you? God, how much longer is this going to take?" These are all common questions and common experiences, as we have seen in previous chapters. In fact, David, in many of the other psalms he wrote, expressed similar feelings;

he questioned whether God knew where he was and what was happening to him.

But here in Psalm 40, David said, "I waited patiently" (v. 1a). On the surface, there seems to be a contradiction to what David is saying. But waiting patiently does not necessarily mean we have no questions about what is happening in our lives and the world around us. Patience does not even mean that we don't experience some normal and natural human anxiety about our circumstances. When David said that he waited patiently on the Lord, at least part of what he meant was that he continued to trust in God despite his questions and his anxiety, despite the long days and even longer nights of living in a dark, desolate pit of life.

Vietnam War POWs repeatedly tell stories about how their faith in God sustained them for six to nine years as prisoners of war in North Vietnam. In story after story, they talk about their belief that they would eventually go home, and how small bits of Scripture and hymns sung silently sustained them when nothing else could. Just like David, they waited patiently for the Lord, and He again heard their cry and answered. He rescued them and brought them up out of the desolate pit and gave them a new life.

New Song

Just as every story that describes how God rescued a person after waiting patiently for months, even years, ends in celebration, each of those POWs describes the celebrations that happened when they were reunited with family. David went on to describe his own celebration: "He [God] put a new song in my mouth, a hymn of praise to our God" (v. 3a). When God rescues us from dark and desolate periods following traumatic events and long periods of grief and loss; when we come to the place that Brueggemann describes as a new coherence of life; when we can say with Job, "My ears had heard of you but now my eyes have seen you" (Job 42:5 NIV), there is an inevitable celebration.

An Iraq war veteran was riding in a vehicle when it was struck by an IED. He suffered significant burns throughout his body, and was medically evacuated to the US, where he endured months in the hospital and more than thirty surgeries. A year and a half later, his wife spoke about their experiences in their church. She detailed her own emotions upon learning of his injuries. In doing so, she described a supernatural peace that had accompanied her through the worst of the initial impact. She talked about her husband's bravery amid such physical pain. She went on to say that God had accompanied them and provided them with many unexpected blessings, even in the darkest times. Finally, she concluded that they both had come to the realization that God had entrusted them with a significant opportunity to share about His goodness and His presence as a result of all that they had been through. Like David, they had a new song about God in their hearts. Like many others, they could say, "God, I only *thought* I knew about You before all this. Now . . . now, I *really* know You." They spoke about their experiences, not because they wanted to celebrate the bad things that had happened, but because they wanted everyone to know about God's loving presence with them through every step of their journey—through the hardest days and longest nights. They wanted people to know about God's amazing love and His steadfast presence; that they had called out to Him, and He heard their cry, and answered. He rescued them and gave them a new life in the aftermath of their suffering, and they wanted everyone to know about it!

David's desire was not just to sing about God's goodness, he wanted other people to know how good God had been to him throughout his lifetime. Notice what he says after he describes the new song that God had put on his lips: "Many will see and fear, and they will trust in the LORD" (Ps. 40:3b). For many who experience trauma, the questions dominate everything! They take on a life of their own and, for many people, become the reason that they lose faith in God. They become bitter and isolated people, angry at God and the world around them. It is easy to see how this could be the case. There is much darkness in our world, and pain and suffering abound.

David wrote about his experiences and emotions so that we might be able to see God's goodness through his suffering; that we might ultimately be able to make friends with the darkness that descends upon each of our lives; that we might be able to tell our own stories of God's rescue—how we waited patiently for Him to answer, and how He heard our cries for help and responded.

The final chapter in our traumatic suffering should never be about the pain itself, but the story of how God was with us through the journey, so that others can find help too. But ultimately, God's rescue is about more than our traumatic experiences and the grief and loss associated with them. It is not enough to find healing and wholeness for this life alone. When Christians read: "He brought me up from a desolate pit, out of the muddy clay, and set my feet on a rock, making my steps secure" (v. 2), it is through the lens of Jesus Christ. This passage refers not only to the temporal rescue of God in the circumstances of life, as David described, but these words also describe the work of the eternal redemption provided by Jesus Christ as He died on the cross for the sin of all humanity.

The Bible teaches that humanity is separated from God because of our sin. We are born into a world that has turned its back on God from near the beginning of time. We also each add to that rebellion in large and small ways, ironically creating more trauma for others along the way. As a result, we are banished from God's presence and deserve eternal separation from Him in a very real place called hell. The good news is that while we were powerless to do anything about our eternal situation, God heard our collective cries and answered. He came to earth as one of us, in the person of Jesus Christ. He lived the perfect, sinless life that none of us ever could. Then, as Jewish Messiah, He sacrificed Himself on the cross as a once-for-all-time Passover Lamb, for the sin of humanity, crying out at His death that our sin was paid in full. Then, three days later, He got up and walked out of the tomb to prove that He had authority to forgive sin as well as authority over death and hell.

He invites each of us into a relationship with Him as a result. Such a relationship requires a few things: (1) that we become humble enough to admit that we have sinned and that we need His forgiveness; (2) that we believe in Him and that what He did on the cross was enough to provide eternal forgiveness for our sin; and (3) that commit to following Him for the rest of our lives.

Unfortunately, stubborn refusal to enter such a relationship with God, paid for by the blood of Jesus, means that you remain separated from God, and upon your death will spend eternity in hell. I can think of no worse tragedy than to experience trauma, grief, and loss while on earth and then never experience God's redemptive activity in this life or in the one to come. The good news is a that way has been made for you to reunite with God, to trust and follow Him.

David said:

> I waited patiently for the LORD, and he turned to me and heard my cry for help. He brought me up from a desolate pit, out of the muddy clay, and set my feet on a rock, making my steps secure. He put a new song in my mouth, a hymn of praise to our God. Many will see and fear, and they will trust in the LORD. (Ps. 40:1–3)

Will this be your story? Or will you pass on God's offer? The stakes could not be higher. Please trust God for your own sake, then tell others how God came to your rescue.

The American poet Robert Frost wrote of coming to a crossroads in life, when a decision must be made. Some have speculated that Frost wrote about contemplating a decision to follow God. Nevertheless, the decision lies before each human being to choose to believe and accept God's love and forgiveness or reject it.

> Two roads diverged in a yellow wood,
> And sorry I could not travel both
> And be one traveler, long I stood
> And looked down one as far as I could
> To where it bent in the undergrowth;
>
> Then took the other, as just as fair,
> And having perhaps the better claim,
> Because it was grassy and wanted wear;
> Though as for that the passing there
> Had worn them really about the same,
>
> And both that morning equally lay
> In leaves no step had trodden black.
> Oh, I kept the first for another day!
> Yet knowing how way leads on to way,
> I doubted if I should ever come back.
>
> I shall be telling this with a sigh
> Somewhere ages and ages hence:
> Two roads diverged in a wood, and I—
> I took the one less traveled by,
> And that has made all the difference.[27]

Choose to let your story end with a glimmer of hope and light.

Epilogue

WHILE I WILL LIKELY NEVER meet most who will read this book, please know that I am praying that God will use our time together through these chapters in a way that brings you hope and refreshment, along with the knowledge that God has not abandoned you. In fact, He knows you and loves you and wants to bring about something meaningful as a result of your tragedy.

On a personal note, I'm proud of you! These chapters have not been easy to read. The work that you have done alongside reading this book, either with a therapist or group, has probably been one of the most emotionally challenging things you have ever done. You have begun a journey to deal with your trauma, rather than letting your trauma deal with you. While this book is complete, your journey is not. Keep talking to friends, keep rereading some of the reflection exercises, stay engaged with those who will continue to challenge you, find a healthy church to attend, and keep talking to God about all of this, no matter what.

Appendix

Definitions

For the purpose of education and reference, the following are definitions of some clinical terms used in this book.

Moral Injury

There is no universally accepted definition of moral injury. However, the following are some of the most prominent working definitions:

- "perpetrating, failing to prevent, bearing witness to, or learning about acts that transgress deeply held moral beliefs and expectations."[28]
- "moral injury is:
  - A betrayal of what's right.
  - by someone who holds legitimate authority (e.g., in the military—a leader).
  - in a high stakes situation.
  - All three."[29]

Post-Traumatic Stress Disorder (PTSD)[30]

A. Exposure to actual or threatened death, serious injury, or sexual violence in one (or more) of the following ways:
 1. Directly experiencing the traumatic event(s).
 2. Witnessing, in person, the event(s) as it occurred to others.
 3. Learning that the traumatic event(s) occurred to a close family member or friend. In cases of actual or threatened death of a family member or friend, the event(s) must have been violent or accidental.
 4. Experiencing repeated or extreme exposure to averse details of the traumatic event(s) (e.g., first responders collecting human remains; police officers repeatedly exposed to the details of child abuse).

B. Presence of one (or more) of the following intrusion symptoms associated with the traumatic event(s), beginning after the traumatic event(s) occurred:
 1. Recurrent, involuntary, and intrusive distressing memories of the traumatic event(s).
 2. Recurrent distressing dream in which the content and/or effect of the dream are related to the traumatic event(s).
 3. Dissociative reactions (e.g., flashbacks) in which the individual feels or acts as if the traumatic

event(s) were recurring. (Such reactions may occur on a continuum, with the most extreme being a complete loss of awareness of present surroundings.)
4. Intense or prolonged psychological distress at exposure to internal or external curse that symbolize or resemble an aspect of the traumatic event(s).
5. Marked physiological reactions to internal or external cues that symbolize or resemble an aspect of the traumatic event(s).

C. Persistent avoidance of stimuli associated with the traumatic event(s), beginning after the traumatic event(s) occurred, as evidenced by one or both of the following:
1. Avoidance of or efforts to avoid distressing memories, thoughts, or feelings about or closely associated with the traumatic event(s).
2. Avoidance of or efforts to avoid external reminders (people, places, conversations, activities, objects, situations) that arouse distressing memories, thoughts, or feelings about or closely associated with the traumatic event(s).

D. Negative alterations in cognitions and mood associated with the traumatic event(s), beginning or worsening after the traumatic event(s) occurred, as evidenced by two (or more) of the following:

1. Inability to remember an important aspect of the traumatic event(s) (typically due to dissociative amnesia and not to other factors such as head injury, alcohol, or drugs).
2. Persistent and exaggerated negative beliefs or expectations about oneself, others, or the world (e.g., "I am bad," "No one can be trusted," "The world is completely dangerous," "My whole nervous system is permanently ruined").
3. Persistent distorted cognitions about the cause or consequence of the traumatic event(s) that lead the individual to blame himself/herself or others.
4. Persistent negative emotional state (e.g., fear, horror, anger, guilt, or shame).
5. Markedly diminished interest or participation in significant activities.
6. Feelings of detachment or estrangement from others.
7. Persistent inability to experience positive emotions (e.g., inability to experience happiness, satisfaction, or loving feelings).

E. Marked alterations in arousal and reactivity associated with the traumatic event(s), beginning or worsening after the traumatic event(s) occurred, as evidenced by two (or more) of the following:
1. Irritable behavior and angry outbursts (with little or no provocation) typically expressed as

verbal or physical aggressions toward people or objects.
2. Reckless or self-destructive behavior.
3. Hypervigilance.
4. Exaggerated startle response.
5. Problems with concentration.
6. Sleep disturbance (e.g., difficulty falling or staying asleep or restless sleep).

F. Duration of the disturbance (Criteria B, C, D, and E) is more than 1 month.
G. The disturbance causes clinically significant distress or impairment in social, occupational, or other important areas of functioning.
H. The disturbance is not attributable to the physiological effects of a substance (e.g., medication, alcohol) or another medical condition.

Notes

1. This description comes from Walter Brueggemann, *The Psalms: The Life of Faith* (Augsburg Fortress Press, 1995), 9–13. For those interested in this categorization of Psalms, the following is a helpful excerpt. Brueggmann proposed "that the sequence of orientation-disorientation-reorientation" is a helpful way to understand the use and function of the Psalms. Very likely, the overview suggested here has been intentional in the practice of many believing people, even though they have not recognized or articulated it in this way.
    1. *The Psalms of Orientation*: The mind-set and worldview of those who enjoy a serene location of their lives and are characterized by a sense of the orderliness, goodness and reliability of life . . .
    2. *The Psalms of Disorientation*: The psalms of lament, both individual and corporate, are ways of entering linguistically into a new distressful situation in which the old orientation has collapsed . . . some of the psalms remember better times . . . back in the old period of orientation. There is a wish to return . . . Others are heavy in anger and resentment against the one who has caused the disorientation. . . . This mood leaves the impression that the speaker believes that the loss of orientation is reversible and the old orientation is retrievable.

> 3. *The Psalms of Reorientation*: A newness has been given that is not achieved, not automatic, and not derived from the old, but rather is a genuine newness wrought by gift. . . . The function speaks of surprise and wonder, miracle and amazement, when a new orientation has been granted to the disoriented for which there was no ground for expectation.

These psalms reflect a quite new circumstance that speak of newness (it is not the old revived); surprise (there was no ground in the disorientation to anticipate it); and gift (it is not done by the lamenter) . . . the power, vitality, and authority for celebration come from the unarguable experience of those persons who have discovered that the world has come to an end but a new creation is given. Life has disintegrated but has been formed miraculously again (emphasis added).

2. The concept of this scenario is taken from the movie *Clear and Present Danger*, directed by Phillip Noyce (Paramount Pictures, 1994), based on the Tom Clancy novel of the same name.

3. The story comes from the TV show, "Young Sheldon," Season 1, Episode 3, "Poker, Faith, and Eggs."

4. Popular Bible translations rendering the passage this way include the New King James Version (NKJV), the New International Version (NIV), the English Standard Version (ESV), as well as several others. The most familiar rendering comes from the 1611 translation, known as the King James Version (KJV): "why hast thou forsaken me?"

5. Word "refuge," *Oxford Dictionary*, https://www.oed.com/dictionary/refuge_n?tab=meaning_and_use.

6. G. A. F. Knight, *Psalms: Volume 1*, "The Daily Study Bible (Old Testament)," ed. John C. L. Gibson (Westminster Press, 1982), 221–22.

7. Jim Michaels, *A Chance in Hell: The Men Who Triumphed Over Iraq's Deadliest City and Turned the Tide of War* (St. Martin's Press, 2010).

8. Dr. Louis DiMarco, "The Battle of Ramadi, 2006–2007," lecture, https://mwi.westpoint.edu/the-battle-of-ramadi-2006-2007/ or https://doleinstitute.org/event/the-battle-of-ramadi-2006/.

9. Abraham Maslow, "A Theory of Human Motivation," *Psychological Review*, 1943.

10. Carey H. Cash, *A Table in the Presence: The Dramatic Account of How a U.S. Marine Battalion Experienced God's Presence Amidst the Chaos of the War in Iraq* (W Publishing Group, 2004), 24.

11. N. Duncan Sinclair, *Horrific Traumata: A Pastoral Response to the Post-Traumatic Stress Disorder* (Haworth Press, 1993), 66.

12. *The Martian*, directed by Ridley Scott (20th Century Studios, 2015).

13. *Groundhog Day*, directed by Harold Ramis (Columbia Pictures, 1993), is a comedy in which the main character Phil (played by Bill Murray) is caught in a cycle of reliving the same day over and over until he, essentially, becomes a better person. The film reference is synonymous with the idea of being stuck in a situation where nothing ever changes.

14. The Anbar Awakening was the result of US relationships built with a number of Iraqi sheiks who led the people of Anbar Province, with the assistance of Iraqi Security Forces (ISF), to turn against and defeat Al-Queda in Iraq.

15. Viktor E. Frankl, *Man's Search for Meaning* (Beacon Press, 1959), 66.

16. Genesis 24

17. Exodus 14

18. Numbers 14–33

19. Exodus 20, 24

20. Charles Haddon Spurgeon, "A Happy Christian," Sermon No. 736 delivered at The Metropolitan Tabernacle, Newington, 1867, https://www.spurgeon.org/resource-library/sermons/a-happy-christian/#flipbook/.

21. Popular Bible translation rendering the passage this way is the New King James Version (NKJV).

22. Elisabeth Kübler-Ross, *On Death and Dying: What the Dying Have to Teach Doctors, Nurses, Clergy and Their Own Families* (Collier Books/Macmillan Publishing, 1970).

23. Sinclair, *Horrific Traumata*, 66.

24. Charles R. Figley and William P. Nash, eds., *Combat Stress Injury: Theory, Research, and Management* (Routledge, 2007), 53.

25. Brueggemann, *The Psalms*, 22.

26. Some readers of this book serve in professions (such as the military, health care, and first responders) that expose you to traumatic events far more frequently over the course of your career than the general public. It may be helpful to have that awareness and seek appropriate support.

27. Robert Frost, "The Road Not Taken," *Atlantic Monthly* (August 1915), https://www.theatlantic.com/magazine/archive/1915/08/the-road-not-taken/645332/.

28. Brett T. Litz, Nathan Stein, Eileen Delaney, Leslie Lebowitz, William P. Nash, Caroline Silva, Shira Maguen, "Moral Injury and Moral Repair in War Veterans: A Preliminary Model

and Intervention Strategy," *Clinical Psychology Review* (2009), quoted in Shira Maguen and Brett Litz, "Moral Injury in Veterans of War," *PTSD Research Quarterly*, vol. 23, no. 1 (2012), 1.

29. Jonathan Shay, "Moral Injury," *Psychoanalytic Psychology*, vol. 31, no. 2 (2014), 183.

30. American Psychiatric Association, *Diagnostic and Statistical Manual of Mental Disorders*, 5th ed. (American Psychiatric Association, 2013).

About the Author

Nick Hamilton served as a chaplain for twenty-five years, first in the military and then after retirement from the Navy, in health care. As the director of spiritual care for Baptist Health of Central Alabama, he led a team of eleven chaplains through the COVID-19 pandemic. As a Navy chaplain, he served on an aircraft carrier on 9/11, deployed to Iraq with Marine Corps ground forces, and served as the chaplain inside the Guantanamo Bay detention facility. He holds a Doctor of Ministry from Gateway Seminary, where he has taught courses on crisis ministry and spiritual formation. Nick is a Board-Certified Chaplain (BCC) and a Healthcare Ethics Consultant—Certified (HEC-C). He currently serves as the director of ethics at Mercy Hospital in Oklahoma City. Nick and his wife, Karen, have three children and two grandchildren.